# GERMANY FOR TOURISTS

The Traveler's Guide to Make The Most Out of Your Trip to Germany - Where to Go, Eat, Sleep & Party

By Dagny Taggart

© Copyright 2015

All rights reserved. No portion of this book may be reproduced -mechanically, electronically, or by any other means, including photocopying- without the permission of the publisher.

**Disclaimer**

The information provided in this book is designed to provide helpful information on the subjects discussed. The author's books are only meant to provide the reader with the basics travel guidelines of a certain location, without any warranties regarding the accuracy of the information and advice provided. Each traveler should do their own research before departing.

# Table of Contents

**MY FREE GIFT TO YOU!** .................................................................... 7

**\* \* \* LEARN GERMAN BEFORE YOU LEAVE - 300% FASTER! \* \* \*** ................ 8

**INTRODUCTION: ARE YOU READY FOR AN ADVENTURE? WELCOME TO GERMANY!** .................................................................................. 9

    WHAT THIS TRAVEL GUIDE CAN OFFER YOU .................................... 9
    IN CASE YOU WANT TO LEARN MORE ............................................ 10

**CHAPTER 1: SETTING EVERYTHING UP BEFORE YOU LEAVE** ........................ 11

    PACKING EVERYTHING YOU NEED FOR YOUR TRAVEL (PART I) ................ 11
    PACKING FOR YOUR TRAVEL (PART II): PACKING THE ESSENTIALS ........... 12
    PACKING FOR YOUR TRAVEL (PART III): CHECKING WITH THE AIRLINES ..... 12
    PLANNING YOUR TRIP ............................................................. 13
    SCHEDULING A CROSS COUNTRY TOUR OF GERMANY - PART I: GETTING ENOUGH REST 13
    SCHEDULING A CROSS COUNTRY TOUR OF GERMANY - PART II: ALLOWING TIME FOR TRAVEL ........................................................................ 14
    THE BENEFITS OF STAYING IN ONE PLACE ..................................... 14
    BOOK YOUR TICKETS EARLY ...................................................... 15
    BRUSH UP ON THE LANGUAGE .................................................... 15
    LEARN THE CURRENCY ............................................................ 16
    UNDERSTAND THE CLOCK ......................................................... 16

**CHAPTER 2: GENERAL OVERVIEW OF GERMANY AND ITS SECTIONS** ............ 17

    THE BEGINNINGS OF A GREAT COUNTRY ....................................... 17
    THE ESTABLISHMENT OF THE GERMAN CONFEDERATION ...................... 18
    CONFLICT AND RESOLUTION ..................................................... 18
    GERMANY TODAY .................................................................. 19
    INDUSTRY AND ECONOMY ........................................................ 19
    CULTURE ............................................................................ 20
    RELIGION ............................................................................ 21

**CHAPTER 3: A CRASH GUIDE TO UNDERSTANDING GERMANS' DAILY LIVES** ................................................................................. 22

- Urban Living .................................................................................................. 22
- Public Transportation .................................................................................. 23
- Cuisine: Food ............................................................................................... 23
- Cuisine: Beverage ........................................................................................ 25
- Sports ........................................................................................................... 25
- Holidays ....................................................................................................... 26

## CHAPTER 4: THE MAJOR REGIONS OF GERMANY ............................ 27

- The 16 States Of Germany ......................................................................... 27
- The Rivers Of Germany .............................................................................. 31

## CHAPTER 5: LET'S GO TO BERLIN ............................................................ 33

- Cultural Institutions - Museums ................................................................. 33
- Cultural Institutions - Performing Ensembles ........................................... 36
- Places To Eat ................................................................................................ 37
- Places To Stay .............................................................................................. 41

## CHAPTER 6: MOVING TO... FRANKFURT! ............................................. 45

- Cultural Institutions - Museums ................................................................. 45
- Places To Eat ................................................................................................ 46
- Places To Stay .............................................................................................. 48

## CHAPTER 7: MAJOR CITIES YOU CAN'T MISS- HAMBURG ............ 53

- Cultural Institutions - Museums ................................................................. 53
- Places To Eat ................................................................................................ 54
- Places To Stay .............................................................................................. 56

## CHAPTER 8: MAJOR CITIES YOU CAN'T MISS - MUNICH ................ 61

- Cultural Institutions - Museums ................................................................. 61
- Places To Eat ................................................................................................ 62
- Places To Stay .............................................................................................. 64

## CHAPTER 9: MAJOR CITIES YOU CAN'T MISS- COLOGNE ............. 69

- CULTURAL INSTITUTIONS - MUSEUMS .......................................... 69
- PLACES TO EAT ........................................................................... 70
- PLACES TO STAY ......................................................................... 73

## CHAPTER 10: MAJOR CITIES YOU CAN'T MISS- STUTTGART ........................ 77

- CULTURAL INSTITUTIONS - MUSEUMS .......................................... 77
- PLACES TO EAT ........................................................................... 78
- PLACES TO STAY ......................................................................... 79

## CHAPTER 11: MAJOR CITIES YOU CAN'T MISS - DRESDEN ........................... 83

- CULTURAL INSTITUTIONS - MUSEUMS .......................................... 83
- PLACES TO EAT ........................................................................... 83
- PLACES TO STAY ......................................................................... 85

## CHAPTER 12: MAJOR CITIES YOU CAN'T MISS- BREMEN ............................. 88

- CULTURAL INSTITUTIONS - MUSEUMS .......................................... 88
- PLACES TO STAY ......................................................................... 88

## CONCLUSION: AREN'T YOU EXCITED? YOUR JOURNEY BEGINS NOW! ........ 91

## * * * LEARN GERMAN BEFORE YOU LEAVE - 300% FASTER! * * * ................ 93

## PS: CAN I ASK YOU A QUICK FAVOR? ....................................................... 94

## PREVIEW OF "GERMAN FOR TOURISTS - THE MOST ESSENTIAL GERMAN GUIDE TO TRAVEL ABROAD, MEET PEOPLE & FIND YOUR WAY AROUND - ALL WHILE SPEAKING PERFECT GERMAN!" ................................................. 95

## CHECK OUT MY OTHER BOOKS ............................................................. 102

## ABOUT THE AUTHOR .......................................................................... 103

*Dedicated to those who love going beyond their own frontiers.*

*Keep on traveling,*

*Dagny Taggart*

# My FREE Gift to You!

As a way of saying thank you for downloading my book, I'd like to send you an exclusive gift that will revolutionize the way you learn new languages. It's an extremely comprehensive PDF with 15 language hacking rules that **will help you learn 300% faster, with less effort, and with higher than ever retention rates**.

This guide is an amazing complement to the book you just got, and could easily be a stand-alone product, but for now I've decided to give it away for free, to thank you for being such an awesome reader, and to make sure I give you all the value that I can to help you succeed faster on your language learning journey.

**To get your FREE gift, go to the link below, write down your email address and I'll send it right away!**

**>> http://bit.ly/GermanGift<<**

GET INSTANT ACCESS

## Learn German Before You Leave - 300% FASTER!

### >> Check Out The Most Awarded German Online Course In Existence (with Audio Lessons!) <<

Wouldn't it be great to learn German before your trip begins? Indeed, it would. Now, let me ask you: what if you could learn it extremely *fast*?

If you truly want to learn German 300% FASTER, then hear this out.

I've partnered with the most revolutionary language teachers to bring you the very best German online course I've ever seen. It's a mind-blowing program specifically created for language hackers such as ourselves. It will allow you learn German 3x faster, straight from the comfort of your own home, office, or wherever you may be. It's like having an unfair advantage!

**The Online Course consists of:**

+ 190 Built-In Lessons
+ 99 Interactive Audio Lessons
+ 24/7 Support to Keep You Going

The program is extremely engaging, fun, and easy-going. You won't even notice you are learning a complex foreign language from scratch. And before you realize it, by the time you go through all the lessons you will officially become a truly solid German speaker.

Old classrooms are a thing of the past. It's time for a language revolution.

If you'd like to go the extra mile follow the link, and let the revolution begin!

>> http://www.bitly.com/German-Course <<

**CHECK OUT THE COURSE »**

# Introduction
## Are You Ready for an Adventure? Welcome to Germany!

Whether you're planning your first trip to Europe or have extensive experience wandering throughout this fascinating continent, a visit to Germany is guaranteed to be a thrilling adventure for all who are interested in immersing themselves in the heartland of Europe!

Featuring scenic natural vistas, bustling cities, historical artifacts and cutting-edge artwork, **Germany is truly a micro-chasm of all that Europe has to offer.** This guide has been designed as a brief introduction to some of Germany's most interesting and popular attractions. Whatever your time constraints or budget preferences may be, we guarantee that you will find something that interests you in this book!

No matter where you've decided to travel to, it's extremely helpful to plan your journey thoroughly before departure. Taking time to make a packing list, reserve transportation, accommodation and event tickets, or simply to learn more about local language and culture will ensure that you have the best possible experience while abroad. **A vacation to Germany will truly be a wonderful excursion!**

What This Travel Guide Can Offer You

The best information comes from those who have truly "been there, done that", just like us! This guide is a combination of first-hand experience and extensive research which has helped it to become a definitive guide for the casual travelers taking their first steps into Europe. This book will ensure that you have all of the information you need to plan an unforgettable vacation, some of which can't be found anywhere else! If you've ever felt uncomfortable or unsure about traveling to Germany, we are confident that this guide will ensure that you are able to have a thrilling and wonderful vacation abroad!

*In Case You Want To Learn More*

If, after reading this guide, you're still interested in learning more about a specific venue, hotel, destination, etc., we highly recommend that you send an email to the particular organization in question. Typically, businesses or institutions that cater to tourists on a regular basis will have a system in place to answer any questions you may have about them.

If any of your friends or family members have traveled to Germany previously, it may be worth taking the time to ask them more about their own travels. **Never underestimate the power of a friendly recommendation.** You may discover an amazing restaurant, café or local attraction that you never even knew existed!

If you're traveling alone, always make sure that you know where embassies and hospitals are in each of the cities you are visiting. **In case of an unexpected emergency, it's absolutely essential that you know how to take of yourself!**

# Chapter 1
## Setting Everything Up Before You Leave

The topics discussed in this chapter include:

- **How to pack for a European vacation.**

- **How to plan a comprehensive trip through Germany.**

### Packing Everything You Need For Your Travel (Part I)

Depending on what your interests are on your upcoming vacation, you may need to approach your packing from one of two distinct perspectives.

**If you're planning on visiting only one city, for example, you may be able to get away with packing larger, less transportable bags.** If you're goal is to live the luxurious life while abroad, you'll probably be providing extra space in your luggage for evening wear and other formal attire.

**That being said, if you're more interested in exploring the country at large, it is absolutely essential that you pack light and prepare yourself for quite a bit of luggage hauling.** The vast majority of European hotels were designed well before the advent of more modern hospitality devices, such as large elevators. Therefore, if you reserve a room on the fourth floor of a boutique hotel, for example, you should probably be prepared to carry your baggage up and down the stairs!

**It's also important for you to carefully consider what type of transportation you will be using during your stay.** If you're only planning on traveling around a large city, like Berlin or Frankurt, for example, it's likely that you can leave the vast majority of your belongings in the hotel while you wander to and from the numerous museums and cultural centers found here. That being said, if you're using the national rail service to commute between various destinations across the country, you'll find that a smaller, more lightweight bag will save you both time and much-needed physical energy. As a general rule of thumb, think of this simple statement when packing for your trip:

**If you can't carry your luggage comfortably, don't bring it with you!**

Packing For Your Travel (Part II): Packing The Essentials

**Knowing what to bring on your European travels can often be confusing, particularly if you've never traveled to this region of the world before.** Before getting caught up in the nitty gritty details of what accessories you should bring and what the perfect German "look" is, it's important to make sure that you have all of the essentials on hand. On Day #1 of your packing process, check to make sure you have these items:

- Passport
- contact information for US embassy / hospitals
- city maps
- cash (either converted to the EU dollar or in your home currency)
- all electronic chargers that you will need to keep your computer / cellphone powered

After you've covered these essentials, you can begin to explore all of your options regarding shoes, clothes, cosmetics etc. Keep in mind that, if you're not on an overly tight budget, you may want to save room in your suitcase for any clothes you find that you would like to buy during your travels. European fashion is often very trendy, and many travelers find that they would like to bring items back home with them from this "fashion-forward" area of the world!

Packing For Your Travel (Part III): Checking With The Airlines

International air travel has changed dramatically in recent years. **In an effort to squeeze a few extra pennies out of air travelers, airlines are now charging passengers for luggage that exceeds relatively stringent weight and size requirements.** Although you may feel tempted to lug an excessive amount of clothing, technology etc., on your adventure, the chances are good that you will end up paying for it!

Before booking your ticket, take a few moments to properly research the baggage rules outlined in the website of your preferred airline. Airline policies regarding the allowable volume of luggage and penalties associated with additional items exceeding these amounts will often vary widely. It is definitely within your best interest to double check these guidelines before you book your ticket in order to ensure that you know exactly what you are getting into!

After you've purchased your ticket and begun the packing process, it may be worth your while to weigh your bags repeatedly throughout the packing process in order to ensure that you don't exceed your designated weight maximum. The last thing you want to have to do is repack all of your bags at the very last minute in order to avoid lofty checked bag fees!

## Planning Your Trip

**What is the ultimate goal of your trip?** Are you passionate about getting a truly in-depth perspective on one location, or are you more interested in surveying all that Germany has to offer, albeit briefly? **How you answer this question is guaranteed to significantly affect how you arrange both your packing and your itinerary for your trip.** Here are a few things to think about when scheduling either type of vacation.

### Scheduling A Cross Country Tour Of Germany - Part I: Getting Enough Rest

When you're sitting in your kitchen at home planning your upcoming vacation, it's almost inevitable that your Google search will turn up dozens of absolutely breathtaking natural landmarks and fascinating cultural hotspots. Although it is obviously recommended that you try to see all that you can during your adventure, it's important to remember that you'll have a few factors working against you during your travels that may leave you extremely fatigued, one of the most annoying being the international travel phenomenon known as jet lag.

Jet lag occurs when a traveler's circadian rhythms, the biological processes that regulate sleep patterns and ensure that individuals get the rest they need to function properly, are disrupted by a substantial change in location and time zone. **Although you may feel perfectly fine when you land in Germany, there's also a significant chance that you will find yourself feeling drained and incredibly fatigued.**

One of the most common mistakes that first-time European travelers make is not setting aside enough time for rest and recuperation at the beginning of their journey. Instead of immediately jumping on a train when you arrive in Germany or hitting the streets to check out the nearest museum, restaurant or performance, give yourself a chance to rest, eat, and take a shower. If you can manage to get a full night's sleep on the first "real" evening of your travels (i.e. the evening hours of the location you are currently at), there's a great chance that you will wake up the next day feeling rested and fully prepared to explore all that this wonderful country has to offer you!

Scheduling A Cross Country Tour Of Germany - Part II: Allowing Time For Travel

**If you only have few days or weeks to travel, the last thing you want to have happen is to spend the majority of your time sitting on trains traveling between destinations.** For most travelers, time spent out and about amongst the numerous famous destinations in Germany is much more entertaining and worthwhile than lengthy commutes and lofty train fares. Because of this, you may find that spending an increased amount of time in fewer locations is much more enjoyable than rushing between dozens of destinations across the country. Not only will this save you time and energy, but it will allow you to devote more of your financial resources to onsite attractions as opposed to paying to travel from Point A to Point B.

The Benefits of Staying in One Place

No matter how much time you spend in one of Germany's larger cities, it's almost guaranteed that you won't be able to see everything that particular location has to offer. This fact alone is a compelling reason why many individuals choose to limit their European vacations to either a specific region within a country or a single city. Not only will this ensure that you have ample opportunity to dig deep into local culture and history, but it will also provide you with much-needed time to rest and relax.
**As stated previously, opting to stay in one city throughout your trip will also ensure that you are able to save money that would have been spent on transportation fares.** While a single ticket may not seem that expensive, it's important to remember that these fares add up, particularly when you're reserving tickets during the summer months when prices are at their highest!

*Book Your Tickets Early*

No matter how many destinations you decide to visit on your upcoming vacation, it's essential that you book your tickets well in advance in order to ensure that you are able to travel freely to and from your desired locations without having to wait in lengthy ticket lines or change travel plans due to sold-out train compartments.

**Booking your travel tickets early, regardless of whether they are plane tickets or train tickets, will also help ensure that you secure the best possible prices.** As demand for tickets increases, often in the months leading up to summer, it's not uncommon for ticket prices to skyrocket. You can avoid this massively price inflation by booking your tickets at least six months in advance of your departure!

*Brush Up On The Language*

Although English is widely spoken throughout Germany, one of the best ways to annoy or irritate locals is to approach them and ask them a question in English assuming they will understand perfectly what you are saying. Although residents of many of Europe's cities are fully accustomed to tourists, very few appreciate it when tourists approach them and expect them to converse in a foreign language. If your goal is to integrate with local residents as best as possible, then it's highly recommend that you, at the very least, **learn a few conversational catch phrases that will show residents of the locations you are visiting that you respect the fact that this is their home, not yours.** Here are a few of the most common and helpful statements and questions you should learn for your upcoming travels.

| Do you speak English? | **Sprechen Sie Englisch?** | *shprêH*-en zee *êng*-lish? |
|---|---|---|
| What times is it? | **Wie geht es Ihnen?** | vee geyt ês *een*-en? |
| How much does . . . cost? | **Wie viel kostet . . . ?** | vee feel *kos*-tet…? |
| Where do I find . . . ? | **Wo finde ich . . . ?** | voh *fin*-de iH…? |
| Where is…? | **Wo ist…?** | voh ist…? |

## Learn The Currency

Sometimes, when individuals embark upon international vacations, standard logic escapes them. One of the most common examples of this is when tourists purchase an item without adequately understanding the money and simply give a large stack of bills to the merchant they are doing business with, expecting them to make the appropriate change for them. Although there are definitely business owners out there who would treat tourists honestly and fairly in these situations, there are an equal number who, unfortunately, would not.

Fortunately, the Euro dollar is a relatively easy currency to understand and use. The Euro is divided into dollars and cents, just like the US dollar. 100 Euro cents equals one Euro dollar, again, behaving identically to the US dollar.

**If you're still unsure about how foreign currency works, approach this topic with your banker before you leave instead of waiting until you arrive, where you could find yourself taken advantage of by unscrupulous shop owners or locals.**

## Understand The Clock

As is common throughout Europe, Germany typically operates on a 24-hour clock. For those accustomed to the 12-hour system used in the United States and Canada, this arrangement may initially be somewhat confusing. That being said, the conversion process is actually quite easy! For any hour past 12:00, say, for example, 16:30 or 18:00, simply subtract 12 to convert to the appropriate PM value. 16:30, therefore, is equivalent is to 4:30 PM, while 18:00 is equivalent to 6:00 PM.

# Chapter 2
## General Overview of Germany And Its Sections

What you're about to learn:

- The origins and history of Germany.

- How Germany's history can be seen and experienced today.

The Beginnings of a Great Country

Although it would take volumes of text to properly summarize the history of the Germany, **a brief overview of some of the formative events that have shaped the cultural and political landscape of this country may prove to be both insightful and enriching for those planning a vacation here.**

One of the earliest and most decisive events in the history of Germany occurred in 800 AD, when Charlemagne, a Frankish king, was crowned emperor of the Carolingian Empire, a unified body that would soon pave the way for the development of the kingdom of France and the kingdom of

Germany. For the next millennium, German princes would gain various degrees of authority and power, even having one of their own elected to the position of Holy Roman Emperor in 962. In 996, the kingdom of Germany gained further respect and authority when Gregory V was elected to be the first German Pope. Although the kingdom of Germany would continue to expand following expansion efforts in the South and East into Slavic territory, the onset of the Black Death in 1348 led to a severe decline in population.

A pivotal moment in German history occurred in 1517, when Martin Luther challenged the embedded doctrines of the Roman Catholic Church with his famous document, "The Ninety-Five Theses". **Luther's actions are widely credited as the catalyst which led to the Protestant Reformation and the establishment of the Lutheran church, which was embraced by several German states in decades following his historic actions.** Rising religious tensions in Germany led to the onset of the Thirty Years' War, which reduced the population of Germany by nearly 30% and ravaged much of the countryside here.

## The Establishment of the German Confederation

Although Germany was largely fragmented following the conclusion of the Thirty Years' War, it would later experience renewed strength, cohesion and unity following the downfall of Napoleon and the historic Congress of Vienna in 1814, which resulted in the official establishment of the German Confederation, a **collection of 39 sovereign states which would slowly congeal and unify over the course of the next century.**

## Conflict and Resolution

The arrival of the 20th century brought with it a series of devastating armed conflicts, including both the First World War and the Second World War, two major international catastrophes whose respective culminations brought with them a series of heavy-hitting repercussions and reprimands for the country of Germany. That being said, Germany would slowly be rebuilt in the years following the closure of the Second World War and the subsequent collapse of the Berlin Wall in 1989 / 1990 and the subsequent re-unification of East and West German which had previously been divided by the Allied powers following the defeat of the Nazis in the 40's.

Following the creation of the European Union, Germany has rapidly risen in prominence to become one of the most economically stable and powerful countries in the conglomeration today. Germany boasts one of the healthiest economies in the EU and some of the lowest jobless rates on the continent. Because of this, Germany has been able to invest significantly in innovation and culture, making it a must-visit destination for entrepreneurs and artists from all walks of life.

## Germany Today

When exploring the cities and villages prevalent across the country, **it's easy to see just how present Germany's past remains.** As is common with much of Europe, ancient buildings line the streets of German cities alongside newer skyscrapers and office complexes. The extensive religious history of Germany remains ever-present thanks to the abundance of historic churches found throughout the country at large. Although the history of this country has largely been preserved, the German people have also placed significant emphasis on preparing themselves for the future. Today, Germany boasts one of the most diversified and advanced economies and civic infrastructures in all of Europe.

**Whether you are planning on visiting quaint villages along the Rhine River or the advanced urban infrastructure of Munich or Berlin, the balance of "old" and "new in Germany is plain to see!**

## Industry and Economy

**As mentioned in the preceding sections, Germany currently hosts one of the most active and viable economies in the entirety of the European Union.** Given the fact that much of the country was destroyed following the close of the Second World War in the 1940's, the fact that Germany now plays such a leading role in international politics is a testament to both the resolve and the work ethic of the German people.

Currently, Germany boasts the fourth-largest economy in the world in terms of Gross Domestic Product. Additionally, in 2011, Germany was the largest financial contributor to the European Union as a whole. **With 37 of the world's Fortune Global 500 companies headquartered in Germany, it should come as no surprise that the country is considered one of Europe's**

**strongest product and service innovators.** By placing special emphasis on the nurturing and development of small and medium-sized business enterprises, the German government has helped to unsure that an abundance of job opportunities are available to citizens throughout the country. Some of the largest German companies operating today include Volkswagen AG, Daimler AG, Deutsche Bank AG, Deutsche Telekom AG, and BMW AG, as well as several other significant enterprises. Germany currently is the wealthiest country in Europe, and the second richest in the world, behind the United States of America.

**Some of the most important economic contributions that Germany has made to the global landscape are within the realms of technology, research and development.** Germany has invested heavily in environmentally responsible technology and energy production, an industry which experiences an annual turnover of over €200 billion here. Currently, Germany generates energy from a variety of sources, including oil, natural gas, nuclear power, hydro/wind power and bituminous coal, among others.

## Culture

Since its inception, Germany has been considered a cultural hub within the European continent at large, helping this country gain the nickname "Das Land der Dichter und Denker" (the land of poets and thinkers).

**Featuring one of the most well-supported and developed artistic infrastructures in the continent, Germany currently hosts countless museums, symphony orchestras, libraries, galleries, theatres, and other cultural centers.** Many of the world's most renowned artists and creative mind have lived in cities throughout Germany.

Some of the more famous German visual artists include Baroque-era painter Peter Paul Rubens, the Impressionist painter Max Liebermann, as well as noteworthy contemporary artistic collectives and interdisciplinary creators, such as Joseph Beuys, Gerhard Richter and HA Schult.

Western music is largely indebted to the work of several German composers, such as Johann Sebastian Bach, Wolfgang Amadeus Mozart, Franz Schubert, Karlheinz Stockhausen and Carl Orff, among others. These composers are typically featured in symphonic orchestra programs around the world throughout the year.

Notable literary talents in Germany include Theodor Fontane, Johann Wolfgang von Goethe, Thomas Mann, Herman Hesse and the Brothers Grimm. Philosophical writings from German thinkers have also thoroughly embedded themselves within the canon of acclaimed Western thought. Examples include works from Theodor Adorno, Immanuel Kant, Georg Wilhelm Friedrich Hegel and Martin Heidegger, among others.

Although there are, obviously, countless more individuals working within a variety of industries that deserve recognition for their creative brilliance, those listed here may serve as an excellent initial point of inquiry for those hoping to learn more about Germany's fascinating culture before beginning their travels.

## Religion

Germany has an extensive Christian tradition and legacy that can still be seen throughout the country. According to recent statistics, nearly 60% of Germans currently identify themselves as practicing Christians. When considering the fact that the next most popular religion, Islam, is only practiced by 2% of the population, it is plain to see how dominant Christian belief is throughout the country at large.

Although Germany was originally formed under the auspices of the Catholic religion during the reign of the Holy Roman Empire, this rather restrictive foundation was first challenged in the opening years of the 16th century by Martin Luther, whose decisive actions led to the onset of the Protestant Reformation.

National constitutions outlined in 1919 and 1949 guaranteed more protected freedoms for varying faiths and religions practiced by German citizens. Today, a wide variety of religions and spiritual practices can be found throughout Germany. **Although Christianity is the most popular religion here, it by no means the only faith that German individuals support.**

## Chapter 3
## A Crash Guide to Understanding Germans' Daily Lives

What you're about to learn:

- How German citizens live their daily lives.

**One of the most common assumptions that first-time European travelers make about the lifestyles of those who lives on the continent is that they are nearly identical their own.** That being said, travelers from countries such as Canada and the United States may be in for a very big surprise (and a touch of culture shock) when they arrive here! The daily lives of Germany's citizens are reflective of the country's cultural and societal values, some of which may be new to those who have yet to visit this region of the world.

### Urban Living

Within the country of Germany are eleven major urban centers :

- Berlin (est. population - 3.5 million)
- Hamburg (est. population 1.8 million)
- Munich (est. population - 1.4 million)
- Cologne (est. population - 1 million)
- Frankfurt (est. population - 689,000)
- Stuttgart (est. population - 610,000)
- Düsseldorf (est. population - 599,000
- Dortmund (est. population - 581,000)
- Essen (est. population - 575,000)
- Bremen (est. population - 548,000)

**These cities are widely considered to be the economic and cultural hubs of the country at large.** Residents of these cities are common employed in any of several in-demand industries found here. Unlike more rural locations, the most common form of accommodation in these cities is apartment units. Because of this, Germany maintains an actively welcoming atmosphere in its city streets, many of which are filled with shops, restaurants, cafés and other hospitality institutions. Leasing rates in the vast majority of Germany's cities are consistently less expensive than in cities such as New York or London, which commonly rank among the most expensive in world surveys. **Thanks to a relatively affordable cost of living, many of Germany's larger urban centers are capable of hosting a diverse cross-section of individuals whose interests and cultural heritages are widely varying.**

Public Transportation

Public transportation can be found throughout the vast majority of Germany's urban areas. In Berlin, for example, residents and tourists have the option of traveling using trams, taxis, buses, the S-Bahn (overground) trains and the U-Bahn (underground) trains. Because of this, it's relatively easy for citizens of these cities to commute to and from their residences and places of work without the need of a car. Pedestrian traffic is often quite dense in these locations, and there are also a substantial number of individuals who travel using bicycles.

Travel between cities and to various locations throughout the country can also be accomplished using the national rail system, which offers affordable rates for long-distance journeys. For tourists, the Deutsche Bahn (national German rail system) is the ideal method for quickly traveling between many of Germany's more popular destinations. Those who are interested in exploring as many of Germany's must-see destinations are advised to invest in the purchase of a German Rail Pass, which offer affordable discounts for those with extensive travel plans.

Cuisine: Food

There's no shortage of culinary offerings in many of Germany's cities and towns. Although smaller communities are likely to feature more traditional German faire, the larger cities dispersed throughout the country feature a kaleidoscopic array of international delights. The iconic German dinner menu is likely to include a variety of meat-based courses, including:

- Pork (often in sausage form)

- Beef (including braised, pan-fried, and marinated dishes)

- Poultry (including duck, goose, and turkey)

- Fish (Alaskan Pollock being the most common)

Vegetable-based entrées are also common in German kitchens, some of the most popular being stews and soups.   One of the more popular vegetables in Germany is white asparagus, locally referred to as 'spargel'. During prime 'spargel' season, it's not uncommon for restaurants to create special menus devoted to dishes using this delicious offering as a primary ingredient.

For those who may secretly be harboring a sweet tooth, Germany is the place to be! Cakes and tarts are quite popular in many parts of the country, and it's not uncommon to find these delicious offerings in any of the numerous bakeries found throughout the country. Bakers will often incorporate fresh fruits into their pastries, added a layer of complexity and deliciousness that is impossible to resist. One of the most iconic German desserts is Schwarzwälder Kirschtorte, also known as   Black Forest cake, which typically features a rich, whipped cream and cherries.

**It's not uncommon for residents of both the larger cities and smaller communities to divide their time between cooking and eating out with friends and family.** In similar fashion to England, there exists a pervasive "pub culture" in Germany which provides both men and women with a welcoming community complete with warm company and delicious food.

Daily meals are often structured as following:

- **Breakfast** - Unlike the breakfast items that travelers from North America may be accustomed to, the German's often incorporate a variety of deli meats and spreads into their breakfast meals. These are typically accompanied by toast, honey, cheese, tea, coffee and assorted juices.

- **Lunch** - Lunch is often considered a "secondary" meal, as opposed to the larger and more lavish breakfasts and dinners. For working adults, lunch often occurs anytime between the hours of 12 - 2 P.M. Although lunches used to be a more heavy addition to the day's culinary enjoyment, newer trends in healthy eating have overshadowed more traditional "meat and potatoes" -esque lunches. A lunch snack which features vegetables, fruits and some protein is quite typical.

- **Dinner** - Often considered the largest meal of the day, dinner in Germany often consists of meat dishes, cheeses, breads and vegetables. Although the original German dinner, often referred to as "Abendbrot", or evening bread, consisted primarily of whole grain bread and deli meats, many individuals now prepare more lavish, hot dinners instead. Dinner often occurs in the early evening hours, but may vary considerably depending upon the work hours of the individual(s) in question.

## Cuisine: Beverage

**When foreigners think of Germany's culinary traditions, the brewing and drinking of beer often comes to mind.** Although beer is a popular beverage in Germany, consumption of this particular drink has declined in recent years. Mineral water is very popular in Germany, and, combined with tea, are two of the most requested non-alcoholic beverages in the country. Coffee is also prevalent throughout Germany.

The Germans have an extensive winemaking tradition, with some of the world's most popular wine growing regions, such as Pfalz, Mosel and Rheingau, located within their national borders. **Both red and white wine are considered popular alcoholic beverages amongst the German people.**

## Sports

Physical exercise and fitness have long been one of Germany's most popular passions. According to recent studies, 27 million German citizens currently belong to sports clubs located throughout the country. It is also estimated that 12 million residents of Germany pursue sports outside of the club environment on a regular basis.

**As could be expected, football is widely considered to be the most popular sport in Germany.** The top men's football club in Germany, Bundesliga, attracts the second highest number of attendees of any sports league in the world. The German national soccer team recently came into the international spotlight when they won the FIFA 2014 World Cup, a title they have claimed three other times in the last several decades.

**Germany has a gained a reputation for excellence in Olympic sports as well.** With the third-highest overall medal count of any country in the world, Germany is considered a formidable contender in both the Summer Olympics and the Winter Olympics.

Holidays

As is common with many Western nations, holidays celebrated in Germany are often classified as either religious or nationalist in nature. Some of the more popular holidays celebrated in Germany include:

- New Year's Day (January 1)
- Good Friday (two days prior to Easter Sunday)
- Labor Day (May 1)
- Germany Unity Day (October 3)
- Christmas Day (December 25)
- Peace Festival (August 8)

Visitors hoping to catch a colorful glimpse of local tradition and culture are advised to schedule their trips to Germany in time with any one of these holidays.

# Chapter 4
# The Major Regions of Germany

## The 16 States Of Germany

Germany is currently divided into sixteen political states, each of which features a unique capital, government head, reigning government party and coat of arms. **It's important to briefly survey this list of states, if only to provide you with a frame of reference when planning your upcoming travels.**

The German states are as follows:

| State | Capital |
|---|---|
| Baden- Württemberg | Stuttgart |
| Bavaria | Munich |
| Berlin | - |
| Brandenburg | Potsdam |
| Bremen | - |
| Hamburg | - |

| State | Capital |
|---|---|
| Hesse | Westbaden |
| Lower Saxony | Hanover |
| Mecklenburg - Vorpommem | Schwerin |
| North Rhine - Westphalia | Düsseldorf |
| Rhineland - Palatinate | Mainz |
| Saarland | Saarbrücken |
| Saxony | Dresden |
| Saxony - Anhalt | Magdeburg |
| Schleswig - Holstein | Kiel |
| Thuringia | Erfurt |

**Baden-Württemberg**

Located in the southwest region of Germany, Baden-Württemberg is the third largest state in Germany by both size and population. The state's capital, Stuttgart, is widely considered to be one of the most important cities in the country in terms of economic contribution.

**Bavaria**

Posited in the southeast region of Germany, Bavaria is the largest state by size in all of Germany. The capital of Bavaria, Munich, is the third largest city in Germany, and is a prominent cultural and economic center.

**Berlin**

Berlin occupies a unique position within in Germany, serving as both the national capital and one of the 16 states within the country. Berlin is currently the country's largest city by population and the seventh most populated city in the European Union. Berlin's economy is primarily driven by tech-related enterprises and the professional service sector.

**Brandenburg**

Located in the eastern region of Germany, the state of Brandenburg was one of several states that were recreated following the reunification of East Germany and West Germany in 1990. The capital of Brandenburg is Potsdam.

## Bremen

Consisting of two cities, Bremen and Bremerhaven, the state of Bremen is the smallest of the 16 German states. Bremen is located in the northern region of Germany. and is surrounded by the state of Saxony.

## Hamburg

This German state is the 13th largest within the country of Germany and is also the second largest city in the country. Featuring a local population of approximately 1.8 million residents, Hamburg has become one of the largest national transport hubs. Hamburg has also become one of the more prominent media centers in Germany.

## Hesse

The term 'Hesse' applies to both a cultural region of Germany as well as an individual state within the country. The state of Hesse contains nearly six million inhabitants and is centrally located within the country.

## Lower Saxony

Lower Saxony is located in the northwestern region of the country and contains a residential population of approximately eight million inhabitants. The state of Lower Saxony is located within the northwestern region of the country.

## Mecklenburg-Vorpommern

Mecklenburg-Vorpommern is the sixth largest state in the country of Germany and is also its least densely populated. The capital of Mecklenburg-Vorpommern is Schwerin. This German state is located in the northeastern region of the country.

## North Rhine - Westphalia

This particular German state is the most populated in all of Germany and is the fourth largest state in the country by physical size. The capital of North

Rhine - Westphalia is Düsseldorf, and the largest city found here is Cologne. This state is located in the western region of the country.

**Rhineland-Palatinate**

Featuring a local population of slightly over four million residents, Rhineland-Palatinate is located in the southwestern region of the country. The capital city of this state is Mainz.

**Saarland**

Excluding the city-states of Berlin, Hamburg and Bremen, Saarland is the smallest state in Germany by both size and population. Saarland has gained renown for its extensive coal deposits and the dearth of economic activity that occurred here throughout the 20th century.

**Saxony**

The state of Saxony is the 10th largest by size in the country and the 6th largest by population. The capital city of Saxony is Dresden. Approximately 4.3 million residents call Saxony home.

**Saxony - Anhalt**

Saxony-Anhalt is one of several landlocked states located within the country of Germany. Featuring a residential population of nearly 2.3 million, Saxony-Anhalt is the 8th largest state in the country by population and the 10th largest by size. The capital of Saxony-Anhalt is Magdeburg.

**Schleswig-Holstein**

The state of Schleswig-Holstein is the northernmost of all German states. Approximately 2.8 million residents call this area home. The capital of Schleswig-Holstein is Kiel.

**Thuringia**

Centrally located within Germany, the state of Thuringia features a residential population of nearly 2.29 million residents. The capital city of

Thuringia is Erfurt. Thuringia is the sixty smallest state by size and fifth smallest by population within the country.

Each of the German states contains its own distinct culture and heritage, which allows for entertaining and enriching explorations and discoveries for travelers who are able to embark on a comprehensive tour of the country. Although it's impossible to experience all that there is to see in Germany on one trip, savvy travelers can develop a travel plan that ensures they are able to take in a large number of Germany's acclaimed sights!

## The Rivers Of Germany

Geographically speaking, the country of Germany is quite unique due to the fact that rivers located within the national boundaries flow into one of several prominent bodies of water, including the **North Sea, Black Sea and the Baltic Sea.**

The three most important rivers flowing through Germany are:

**The Oder River**

531 miles (854 kilometers) in length, the Oder River, also referred to as the "Odra River", flows through the Czech Republic and Poland before making its way into Germany and, ultimately, emptying into the Baltic Sea.

**The Danube River**

**The Danube River is the European Union's longest river and the second longest within continental Europe.** The Danube River is unique in the fact that it flows through or touches the national borders of 10 countries before emptying into the Black Sea. These 10 countries include Romania, Hungary, Serbia, Austria, Germany, Bulgaria, Slovakia, Croatia, Ukraine, and Moldova.

**The Rhine River**

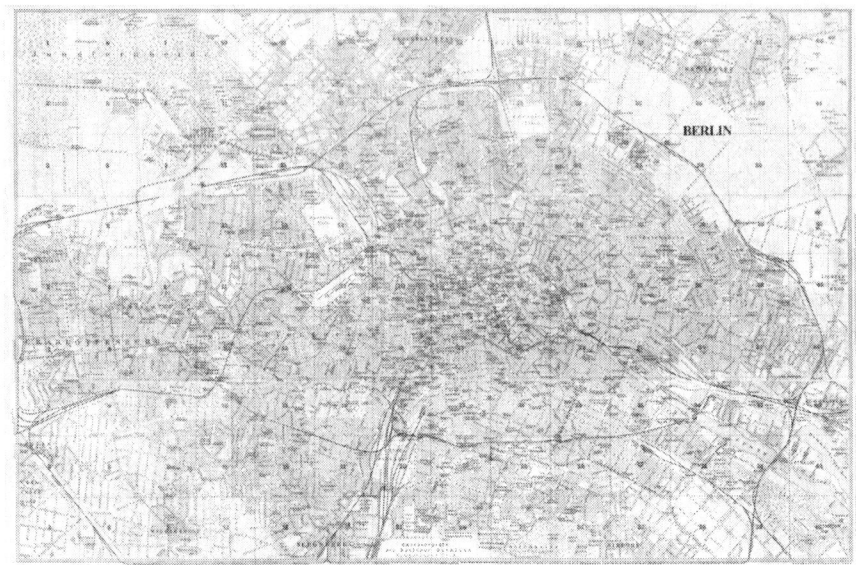

Originating in the Swiss Alps, the Rhine River makes its way through Germany before emptying into the North Sea. The Rhine River is the twelfth longest river in the country, traversing approximately 766 miles. Widely considered to be one of the most important rivers in all of Europe, the Rhine River has long been a sort of vital economic transport for many nations throughout history.

Each of these historic waterways has its own unique legacy and history. Many of Europe's most prominent cities and cultural landmarks are located alongside these vital geographical resources. For those interested in a one-of-a-kind tourism experience, traveling form the origins of any one of these rivers to its mouth is guaranteed to provide unique perspective into the historical development of continental Europe at large.

# Chapter 5
## Let's Go to Berlin

A vacation to Germany is not complete without spending time in **Berlin, the capital of the country and one of the nation's most historically important locations.**

Cultural Institutions - Museums

**The city of Berlin is currently home to more than 130 museums and over 400 art galleries.** Depending upon your specific tastes and aesthetics, there are likely to be numerous venues that focus specifically on your interests. Some of the more renowned museums in Berlin include:

**Alte Nationalgalerie:**

Bodestrasse 1-3

Berlin, Berlin D-10178 Germany

**Website:** http://www.smb.museum/home.html

The Alte Nationalgalerie was first established in 1861, following years of development under the authority of governmental officials. **The original design for this now iconic museum was conceived of by Friedrich August Stüler, who was required to submit three designs for the proposed museum before permission was given to proceed.** The Alte Nationalgalerie focuses primarily on Neoclassical and Romantic-period works. Notable artists whose work can be found in the Alte Nationalgalerie include Caspar David Friedrich, Édouard Manet, Claude Monet, Max Liebermann and Lovis Corinth, among others. **The Alte Nationalgalerie currently contains the largest collection of 19th century sculpture in the entire country.** The museum is suitable for both adults and children, and is typically open throughout the year, barring national holidays.

**Egyptian Museum of Berlin**

Bodestra ße 1-3,

Berlin, Berlin I10178 Germany

Website: http://www.egyptian-museum-berlin.com

A subsidiary of Germany's acclaimed Neues Museum system, the Egyptian Museum of Berlin (Ägyptisches Museum und Papyrussammlung) **contains one of the most important collections of Egyptian art and artifacts in the entire world.** The collection found at the museum features pieces dating back to 4000 BC and culminating in artifacts produced during Roman rule in the area. That being said, the vast majority of exhibition pieces found at the Egyptian Museum of Berlin have been dated to nearly approximately 1340 BC. The museum itself was first established by reigning Prussian kings during the 18th century. Although this particular cultural institution was divided into two distinct cultural entities prior to the fall of the Berlin Wall, the Egyptian Museum was later merged during the historic Reunification of Germany. The museum is suitable for both adults and children, and is typically open throughout the year, barring national holidays.

**Jewish Museum of Berlin**

Lindenstra ße 9-14

Berlin, Berlin 10969 Germany

Website: www.jmberlin.de

**Widely considered to be one of the largest collections of Jewish history and artifacts in all of Europe, the Jewish Museum Berlin currently has over 2,000 years of Jewish history on display.** The museum incorporates a diverse permanent collection, as well as a variety of revolving exhibitions that highlight various aspects of the Jewish experience. The museum was first opened in 2001 and remains one of the most heavily trafficked cultural institutions in the city. In close proximity to the museum is the Academy of the Jewish Museum, which features document archives, a library, the official education department of the museum and a lecture hall. The museum is currently overseen by W. Michael Blumenthal, who was the former Secretary of the Treasury for President Jimmy Carter. The museum was designed by renowned architect Daniel Libeskind. Construction first began on the Jewish

Museum in November, 1992 and was finally completed in 1999. The museum is suitable for both adults and children, and is typically open throughout the year, barring national holidays.

**German Historical Museum**

Unter den Linden 2,

Berlin, Berlin10117 Germany

Website: www.dhm.de/en.html

The German Historical Museum (Deutsches Historiches Museum) is a Berlin-based cultural institution that is primarily devoted to preserving, archiving and exhibiting artifacts and collections related to the history of Germany. Identifying itself as a center of "enlightenment and understanding of the shared history of Germans and Europeans", **the DHM is considered to be one of Berlin's most important museums.** It is also one of the most frequently visited museums in the city. The DHM was first established in 1987 as part of the 750th anniversary celebration of the founding of the city, and was designed by internationally renowned architect I. M. Pei. The museum features over 8,000 square meters of exhibition space which include both permanent and temporary exhibitions, as well as a library and cinema. Items on display at the museum span a wide variety of interests and subject areas, including fine art, military objects, films, historical photographs, documents and posters, among other items. The museum is suitable for both adults and children, and is typically open throughout the year, barring national holidays.

**German Museum of Technology**

Trebbiner Straße 9

Berlin, Berlin 10963 Germany

Website: www.sdtb.de

The German Museum of Technology (Deutsches Technikmuseum Berlin) has made it their goal to chronicle the various scientific and technological achievements made by Germans throughout history. The original emphasis of the German Museum of Technology was the various innovations made in rail transportation, although the institution has since expanded to encompass maritime and aviation-related pursuits as well. Notable items on display here include a thorough collection of rail-related paraphernalia, much of which is sourced from 19th century roundhouses, as well as a variety of vintage airplanes and early electronic equipment. The museum is suitable for both adults and children, and is typically open throughout the year, barring national holidays.

## Cultural Institutions - Performing Ensembles

**Berlin Philharmonic**

Website: http://www.berliner-philharmoniker.de/en/

**Arguably one of the greatest symphonic ensembles in Europe and the world at large, the Berlin Philharmonic has performed masterworks of the symphonic repertoire for audiences across the globe.** First established in 1882, the Berlin Philharmonic has hosted some of classical music's most famous conductors, composers and performers. Notable directors of the Berlin Philharmonic include Herbert von Karajan, Claudio Abbado and Sir Simon Rattle, among others. The Berlin Philharmonic has distinguished itself by promoting the music of both popular historical composers as well as modern masters. The orchestra has been the recipient of eight Grammy awards and six Gramophone awards. The Berlin Philharmonic performs at the Berlin Philharmonie. Those who are interested in attending a concert at the Berlin Philharmonie with the Berlin Philharmonic are advised to book their tickets well in advance, as these shows are often quite popular. The Berlin Philharmonic is suitable for both adults and children alike.

**Deutsche Oper Berlin**

Website: http://www.deutscheoperberlin.de

For fans of opera or staged theatrical works, a visit to the Deutsche Oper Berlin is highly recommended. The Deutsche Oper Berlin was first established in 1912 in Charlottenburg, a previously independent city which has since become one of several districts within Berlin. **The Deutsche Oper Berlin has** hosted some of the world's leading operatic conductors, including **Bruno Walter, Kurt Adler, Jesús López-Cobos and Lorin Maazel, among others.** Although the Deutsche Oper Berlin has experienced its fair share of controversy throughout the 20th century, including the mid-performance death of conductor Giuseppe Sinopoli, the company remains an ever-present fixture within the Berlin arts scene. The company regularly hosts some of the most popular singers and performers, and remains within the upper tier of opera companies worldwide. The Deutsche Oper Berlin performs at the Deutsches Opernhaus, which was originally designed specifically for the ensemble. Those who are interested in attending an event at the Deutsches Opernhaus are advised to book tickets well in advance, as seating is limited for many of the productions here. The Deutsche Oper Berlin is suitable for both adults and children alike.

## Places To Eat

**Katz Orange**

Website: http://www.katzorange.com/en/

*Our opinion:*

Sustainability and fresh cuisine have become buzzwords among discerning diners around the world. **The chefs at Katz Orange have created a unique menu that successfully blends locally sourced ingredients, responsible farming, seasonally fresh products and dishes suitable for both traditional and non-traditional diners.** Simply put, Katz Orange is a must-visit location!

*Taken from the official website:*

"We find ideas for our dishes all over the world in many different cultures. We try to work with regional products wherever we can and our menu is set up according to seasonal availability of ingredients. We are inspired by gourmet cuisine, but no more than by the dishes our mothers and grandmothers love to cook. We work with ingredients that are produced respectfully towards humans, animals and plants. Our menu is kept small, because we like to work with fresh products and want to keep waste as low as we can. Still we try to offer a range of options at any time, from meat to vegan dishes."

**Cuisine: Sustainable, seasonally dependent upscale continental**

**Pauly Saal**

website: paulysaal.com

*Our opinion:*

Pauly Saal has been designed to emulate the classic bistro experience found during the 1920's. With an interior decor that creates an undeniably unique ambience and a variety of fascinating decorative pieces situated throughout, **the atmosphere in Pauly Saal perfectly complements the upscale dining offerings, which include ox steak, crab, sausages and a variety of other continental European staples.**

**Cuisine: Trendy, upscale continental**

**Facil**

Website: facil.de/en

*Our opinion:*

When in Berlin, it's essential that travelers experience the luxury and opulence that this city has the offer while, simultaneously, exploring the cutting-edge aesthetic frontiers that Berlin has become so famous for. Having earned 2 Michelin Stars, **Facil is guaranteed to provide diners with an unforgettable culinary experience that they will be hard-pressed to find anywhere else.**

*Taken from the official website:*

"The FACIL restaurant (2 Michelin stars), located in the heart of Berlin, has been serving elegantly light fare accented by purist luxury and modern avant-garde since July 2001. The FACIL is the perfect place for unconventional gourmets seeking a culinary experience.

Our chef de cuisine is MICHAEL KEMPF. His style of cooking is modern and creative. He uses exclusively fresh and mostly local products. His dishes are subtle and straightforward. The flavors are fine and distinctive."

**Cuisine: Locally inspired, high-end continental**

**Fischers Fritz**

website: facil.de/en

*Our opinion:*

Traditional cuisine will, in the eyes of many diners, forever be an in-demand commodity. At Fischers Fritz, those seeking the best of continental cuisine can dine in an **upscale, luxurious atmosphere that will allow for fabulous conversation and an exquisite evening out on the town.**

*Taken from the official website:*

"Why not pay a visit to Fischers Fritz gourmet restaurant and take a culinary trip into a world of delicious gourmet dishes and fish specialties? Our chef de cuisine Christian Lohse together with his team of chefs, who have been awarded with two Michelin stars for their work at Fischers Fritz, invite you to sample some of their exquisite, finest quality creations in a most exclusive ambience."

**Cuisine: Classic continental**

**Reinstoff**

Website: reinstoff.eu

*Our opinion:*

Just because cuisine is classified as gourmet doesn't mean it has to be old-fashioned! At Reinstoff, a Michelin Star (2) awarded restaurant, **chef Daniel Achilles has created a unique menu that offers a refreshing perspective on the timeless tastes of continental European cuisine.** For those who are willing to spend the money, Reinstoff may be the perfect place to embark upon the culinary adventure of a lifetime.

*Taken from the official website:*

"Reinstoff is a modern gourmet restaurant, awarded with two Michelin stars and 18 Gault & Millau points. The restaurant is located in the historic Edison courtyards in Berlin-Mitte, where Germany's first light bulbs were manufactured decades ago. In this unique surrounding, chef Daniel Achilles and business economist Sabine Demel as well as their service team around maître Jan-Willem Berendsen and sommelier Pascal Kunert offer a gourmet restaurant, which is truly authentic for Berlin. Because Reinstoff is different – independently and therefore exceptionally personally, focused and diverse, inspiring and genuine."

**Cuisine: Classic continental**

**TIM RAUE**

website: tim-raue.com

*Our opinion:*

Although many individuals do not think of Asian cuisine as a popular dining option in Germany, certain restaurants, such as TIM RAUE, are proving otherwise. **The Asian-inspired dining options found here are created using the highest-quality ingredients which ensures bold flavors and a fresh meal.** Meat plays a prominent role in many of the dishes here, which may prove somewhat difficult for vegetarians or vegans.

*Taken from the official website:*

"At the Restaurant TIM RAUE, we serve Asian-inspired cuisine that can be characterized as a blend of Japanese product perfection, Thai aromas, and Chinese culinary philosophy. For this reason, we do not serve side dishes such as bread, noodles, or rice, nor do we use white sugar. Our kitchen also only works with lactose-free dairy products. The use of animal products is one of the cornerstones of our culinary philosophy. Nearly all our dishes contain animal products, which provide the unique variety of flavors.

Vegetarian alternatives are of course available. However, we cannot offer vegan guests the same taste experience."

**Cuisine: Asian inspired, meat-based dishes, trendy**

Places To Stay

**Honigmond Hotel / Garden Hotel**

website: www.honigmond.de

*Our opinion:*

Many individuals travel to Europe to experience the old-world charm that this region of the world has become known for. **At the Honigmond Hotel, travelers can relax in the opulence of 19th century decor that is both exotic and luxurious.** Conveniently located within walking distance of the heart of Berlin, guests staying at the Honigmond hotel have access to all of the amazing sights and sounds of this vibrant city.

*Taken from the official website:*

"Staying at Honigmond, you will experience the elegance and esprit of the closing of the 19th century. Historic charm and fanciful taste unite and create a living experience of the special kind. As your host, we'll be at your disposition during the whole year. Honigmond is situated right in the centre of Berlin, but at the same time it is quiet and peaceful. It includes a limited amount of underground parking lots and an excellent access to public transportation. Enjoy exploring Berlin's centre by foot or with the bikes we offer. Stroll down Friedrichstrasse, discover Hackescher Markt and Museumsinsel. The excellent access to public transportation allows for a trip to Potsdam or Berlin's surroundings."

**Perfect for : Adults, Children, Couples, Families**

**Ackselhaus**

Website: www.ackseulhaus.de

*Our opinion:*

For some travelers, comfort and solace far outweigh the desire for forward-thinking luxury and in-demand, trendy accommodations. For those who are looking for a quiet respite from the bustling energy of Berlin, the Ackselhaus may be the perfect location. **Housed inside a pristine, historic structure, the Ackselhaus offers the best of modern convenience and gilded era warmth.** This hotel is highly recommended.

*Taken from the official website:*

"WE MAKE YOUR STAY IN BERLIN FEEL LIKE BEING AT HOME …A central place to live, sleep and dream. Although the building is located right in the centre of the city, you will find yourself in an oasis of tranquility. Feel the sensation of a real discovery when visiting this meticulously restored Victorian Age building. People from all over the world feel at home and savor the joy of living right there."

**Perfect for : Adults, Children, Couples, Families**

**Ostel**

Website: www.ostle.edu

*Our opinion:*

The 70's and 80's were a turbulent period for Germany, due in large part to the division of Berlin that produced dramatic cultural shifts and changes. **Nowhere can the spirit of this time be recreated better than the Ostel hotel, which prides itself on providing guests with the chance to experience Berlin during its most formative years.**

*Taken from the official website:*

"Go on a trip back in time to the East Berlin of the seventies and eighties. Enjoy the most beautiful East-German room designs in an original GDR "Platten"-building. You will stay in rooms furnished with classics like the "Karat" wall-wardrobe and the multi-function table. Visit our extraordinary hostel near the Ostbanhof in Berlin. We look forward to your visit!"

**Perfect for : Adults, Children, Couples, Families**

**Hotel Albrectsof**

website: www.hotel-albrechstof.de

*Our opinion:*

**The Hotel Albrectsof is one of many institutions in the city that offers visitors the opportunity to immerse themselves in the well-preserved splendors of Berlin's regal history.** The Hotel Albrectsof is widely recommended for those who prioritize luxury and old-world comfort over trendy or cutting-edge accoutrements.

*Taken from the official website:*

"The hotel was founded as a hospice in 1910 thanks to wealthy friends of the Berlin City Mission. Since 1913 it exists in its original size. Let's take a look at the interesting history of the house: it was used for a variety of purposes such as a temporary home for families separated by the German division or one of few secure meeting points for church representatives during state regimentation. It offered space for experiencing a truth that was not visible on the surface for a long time.The most famous guest in this house probably was the civil rights activist Dr. Martin Luther King who sat together with church representatives in the "Hospice at the train station Friedrichstra ße" during his only visit to East Berlin in 1964."

**Perfect for : Adults, Children, Couples, Families**

**Hotel de Rome**

*Our opinion:*

Yet another historic hotel whose history extends back into the divisive period of time prior to the reunification of Berlin, **the Hotel de Rome offers guests an unparalleled level of luxury and comfort,** successfully blending the highest level of modern convenience with subtle, understated remnants of times gone by which, ultimately, prove that the past can indeed live alongside the present.

Website: https://www.roccofortehotels.com/hotels-and-resorts/hotel-de-rome/

*Taken from the official website:*

"Sitting on one of the most important squares in former East Berlin, Hotel de Rome was originally built in 1889 as the headquarters of the Dresdner Bank. Berlin's history exists within the fabric of our building. The bank manager's office is now a suite. The jewel vault is now a swimming pool. The cashier's hall has been transformed into a ballroom. Berlin's best bits are right outside. Museum Island. The vibrant arts scene. Notorious nightlife. Designer shopping. The fascinating monuments to history"

**Perfect for : Adults, Children, Couples, Families**

**Hotel Adlon**

*Our opinion:*

**The Hotel Adlon is, by all accounts, an outstanding representation of just how seriously Berlin takes luxury and the hospitality industry.** Featuring an outstanding array of modern conveniences and a highly trained, courteous staff, the Hotel Adlon is highly recommended for anyone who is willing to pay for an unforgettable hotel experience in one of the city's most respected institutions.

Website: http://www.kempinski.com/en/berlin/hotel-adlon/overview/

*Taken from the official website:*

"Are you looking for the highest level of luxury services, frills above and beyond your expectations? Well, you have found it. The quintessence of five star guest services and facilities awaits you at the legendary Hotel Adlon Kempinski. Our hotel is located in the very heart of Berlin, right next to the famous landmark Brandenburg Gate."

**Perfect for : Adults, Children, Couples, Families**

# Chapter 6 :
# Moving to... Frankfurt!

## Cultural Institutions - Museums

### Städel

Schaumainkai 63, 60596

Frankfurt am Main, Germany

Website:

**The Städel, also referred to as the Städelsches Kunstinstitut und Städtische Galerie, is widely considered to be one of the most developed and important collections of art in the entirety of Germany.** With a collection of nearly 3,000 paintings and well over 100,000 drawings, this museum has become one of the largest collections of fine art in continental Europe. The museum was first founded in 1815, and has since flourished, despite a series of significant setbacks caused by structural damage to the facilities during the Second World War. Noted artists on display at the museum include Jan van Eyck, Sandro Boticelli, Rembrandt van Rijn, and Edgar Degas, among others. A visit to the Städel can serve as an excellent introduction to fine art for children and a refreshing cultural oasis for adults. The museum is typically open on an annual basis, excluding national holidays and other important events.

### Museum für Modern Kunst

Domstra ße 10, 60311

Frankfurt am Main, Germany

**First established in 1981, the Museum für Modern Kunst in Frankfurt has since become a hub of modern art and contemporary art pieces that challenge and reward audiences who are willing to explore unconventional aesthetics, philosophies and creative processes.** The museum has a distinct geometric shape often referred to as a "piece of cake" The "MMK" was designed by renowned architect Hans Hollein, whose works can be seen around the world. The museum features an extensive permanent collection as well as a variety of traveling exhibitions which shed light into a variety of unique and unforgettable artists and artworks. The museum is typically open throughout the year, although closures will often occur on national holidays. A visit to the Museum für Modern Kunst is ideal for both adults and children alike.

Places To Eat

**Restaurant Villa Rothschild**

Website: http://www.kempinski.com/en/frankfurt/villa-rothschild/dining/

*Our take:*

In keeping with this city's knack for luxury and the "finer things" in life, **the Villa Rothschild restaurant offers discerning diners the opportunity to explore a variety of sensual, exotic tastes and flavors that other restaurants purporting to offer "haute" cuisine may be hard pressed to match.** Featuring a staff of some of the best and brightest culinary minds in the city, Villa Rothschild is guaranteed to impress.

*Taken from the official website:*

"A paradise for bon vivants – whether in the Villa Rothschild's Michelin star restaurant, in Tizian's Bar & Brasserie, or with the treasures of our wine cellar, only the best awaits you. An extraordinary ambience, a gourmet culture and exceptional personal service has turned the Villa Rothschild into an oasis for haute cuisine. No other restaurant and bar in the area of Frankfurt can claim to set such high standards.

Experience the history of an exceptional location in combination with the highest culinary quality at the Villa Rothschild Kempinski - a place for connoisseurs, taste craft lovers and pure gourmets. A unique setting, highest gourmet culture and attentive, individual and authentic service do make your visit a special one."

**Cuisine: Eclectic fine dining**

**Villa Merton**

Website: http://www.koflerkompanie.com/en/restaurants_villamerton.html

*Our take:*

Elegance, luxury, and old world sensibilities all come together at the Villa Merton, an icon within Frankfurt's fine dining scene. Featuring an outstanding menu of continental faire created by some of the most talented and respected chefs in the city, **Villa Merton has quickly become one of the most talked about and popular dining establishments here.**

*Taken from the official website:*

"Villa Merton is located in the "diplomat's quarter", an elegant Frankfurt neighborhood. Richard Merton commissioned this building in 1925 as a private mansion in the neo-baroque style. In 2002, The Union International Club built a restaurant in the mansion, which was awarded a Michelin Star in 2003. All rooms open onto the terrace with a beautiful view of the park and its old trees, providing welcoming shade in the summer. It provides an unrivaled ambience for your events, from private parties to business dinners for 2-100."

**Cuisine: Continental fine dining**

**Zarges**

Website: http://www.zarges-frankfurt.com/site/restaurant

*Our take:*

In a bold break-away from traditional "continental luxe" cuisine, chef Girolamo Falco has created **an ambitious fusion of French and Mediterranean cuisine that is guaranteed to turn heads and tease palates.** Although the food at Zarges isn't cheap, it is well worth the price tag! Diners who venture into the evocative ambience of Zarges are guaranteed to have an amazing evening.

*Taken from the official website:*

"Girolamo Falco is native Italian, but has completed the most important stations of his career in France and Germany. Falco stands for an authentic, natural and modern cuisine. Without following fleeting trends and Zeitgeist-extravaganzas, he skillfully combines flavors and textures without letting the essential – the taste - off his eyes. His light, French style with a Mediterranean twist, is based on the combination of simple and exclusive ingredients in quality as well as their careful preparation. Purchase this is real passion. Only the freshest vegetables, only the aromatic fruit, only the tastiest herbs. Also of his meat, fish and cheese suppliers, it requires unyielding unbeatable quality. It would never enter him in the sense of quality compromises. Every day fresh, every day, every day different."

**Cuisine: French - Mediterranean Fusion**

**Restaurant Français**

website: http://www.zarges-frankfurt.com/site/restaurant

*Our take:*

**Simply put, classic cuisine will always be classic, and nowhere is this better experienced than at the Restaurant Français**, one of Frankfurt's most respected and popular luxe dining establishments that seeks to bring classic French cooking to the highest levels of flavor, enjoyment and pleasure. Diners visiting the Restaurant Français will experience the joys of what the world considers to be the most timeless cuisine on the planet.

*Taken from the official website:*

"As a top awarded restaurant-with a Michelin star ,17 out of 20 "Gault Millau" points and continual praises from numerous restaurant critics, the Chef de Cuisine Patrick Bittner has more than proved himself as an excellent Chef and a master in his trade. We are looking forward to welcoming you in our restaurant!"

Places To Stay

**Villa Kennedy**

Website:https://www.roccofortehotels.com/hotels-and-resorts/villa-kennedy/

*Our take:*

In the heart of Frankfurt's bustling financial district and cutting-edge urban living, one of the last things that many travelers expect to find is a hotel as historic, resplendent and opulent as the Villa Kennedy. **Those who do elect to stay here will find themselves surrounded by old-world luxury and charm that will leave them feeling relaxed, pampered and, most importantly, satisfied.**

*Taken from the official website:*

"Frankfurt is both a powerhouse of finance and a paragon of culture. At its very centre sits the finest hotel in this city — Villa Kennedy. Built in 1904 as a grand family home, the building has been immaculately restored and extended. Today, it combines contemporary elegance with old world touches, such as ornate ceilings and the original oak stairs. The three newer wings blend harmoniously with the old Villa Speyer, creating a tranquil courtyard garden in the centre, ideal for alfresco dinner and drinks. Located beside the Main River's myriad museums, our hotel is a short walk from the city's liveliest bars, boutiques and cultural attractions."

**Perfect for : Adults, Children, Couples, Families**

**Jumeirah Frankfurt**

http://www.jumeirah.com/en/hotels-resorts/frankfurt/jumeirah-frankfurt/

*Our take:*

For those who enjoy a bit of adventure and risk-taking when booking their hotel accommodations, the Jumeirah Frankfurt may be a perfect match. Located just moments away from numerous shopping centers and restaurants, Jumeirah offers travelers an enviable location amidst all that Frankfurt has to offer. **Featuring an assortment of unique, one-of-a-kind** crafts and an interior décor that has to be seen to be believed, Jumeirah is truly a stand-out hotel in Frankfurt.

*Taken from the official website:*

"The striking Jumeirah Frankfurt is located right in the heart of the city – just a few steps away from the popular 'Zeil' shopping street and the financial district. Jumeirah Frankfurt offers 218 spacious guest rooms and suites, with amazing views across the city. Just as delightful is this hotel's refreshing approach. From the original artworks by local artist Hartwig Ebersbach throughout the hotel, to the beehives on the roof that produce our own honey, at Jumeirah Frankfurt we do things a little differently. Everything you experience here is a taste of the very best the city can offer, whether you're dining at the fabulous Max on One restaurant, enjoying a Salt Body Massage at Talise Spa, or attending an event in our magnificent Crystal Ballroom. With little touches like your welcome drink and oshibori upon arrival and complimentary Wi-Fi throughout the hotel, everything we do is designed to make your stay a constant delight."

**Perfect for : Adults, Children, Couples, Families**

**Roomers**

http://www.roomers.eu/en/

*Our take:*

**In an effort to stimulate the mind and indulge the senses, the owners of Roomers have created a hotel experience that is truly unlike any other.** With the goal of providing an entirely new, revolutionary sensual experience, Roomers features outstanding amenities and comforts which fully ensure that all guests begin their time here with an open mind and eager spirit. Thanks to a 24-hour concierge service and top-notch hospitality, Roomers has truly raised the bar for its competitors in the city. Ultimately, Roomers is in a class all of its own.

*Taken from the official website:*

"Welcome to the legendary Roomers, where the perception of sensuality is redefined in this Member of Design Hotels™. A place where fantasy soars and the creativity of its guests is perpetually stimulated. Clear lines, structured forms and atmospheric lighting enhance every stay to become an unforgettable experience. The epiphany of burlesque elegance amidst the pulsating life of Frankfurt metropolis – created against all the ordinary standards and tiresome so-called comfort.

Whether it's the 116 Rooms & Suites, the swanky Restaurant, the award-winning Bar or the innovative Spa area – it's always alluring to frolic from dusk 'til dawn in Roomers. The Sky Lounge commands a breathtaking view over Frankfurt's skyline, and the sun-drenched Patio offers the perfect party and chill-out location during fine summer weather. All these, combined with an exquisite all-round service, raise the bar to another level exceeding guests' expectations beyond their own wishes. And that's 24 hours a day."

**Perfect for : Adults, Couples**

**The Pure Hotel**

http://www.the-pure.de

*Our take:*

The Pure Hotel operates with the idea that a hotel should be defined by the service it offers to its guests, not the fancy frills it throws in the lobby. **Thanks to a relatively intimate environment and wide array of unassuming accommodations, guests staying at The Pure Hotel will have the opportunity to unwind and relax without feeling the need to keep up appearances.** For those visiting Frankfurt for the first time, this could prove to be an enticing idea indeed.

*Taken from the official website:*

"Settled? Feel like home in the owner-operated and award-winning "Member of Design Hotel", in which you are not just treated as a guest but as part of the family. The surroundings invite you to relax, the creative and homely feel-good gimmicks attract you to indulge, and the neighborhood and circumjacent places of interest encourage you to sense being home away from home. We feel you – and will make sure to turn your visit into an unforgettable memory in MAINhattan's metropolis."

**Perfect for : Adults, Couples**

# Chapter 7
## Major Cities You Can't Miss- Hamburg

Cultural Institutions - Museums

**Hamburger Kunsthalle**

Glockengie ßerwall, 20095

Hamburg, Germany

Website: www.hamburger-kunsthalle.de/

**With special emphasis places upon painting taking place in Hamburg during the 14th century, the Hamburger Kunsthalle fills a vital niche within both the city and the country at large.** Additional focus is devoted to Flemish and Dutch visual artists from the 16th and 17th century. The museum was erected over a span of six years between 1863 and 1869 by the renowned architects Georg Theodor Schirrmacher and Hermann von der Hude. One of the more notable events that has occurred here in recent years was the theft of a famous painting by renowned artist Caspar David Friedrich, which was later returned to the museum following a somewhat turbulent legal battle. A visit to the Hamburger Kunsthalle is ideal for both adults and children alike.

**Museum of Ethnology Hamburg**

Rothenbaumchaussee 64, 20148

Hamburg, Germany

Website: http://www.voelkerkundemuseum.com

**First established in 1879, Hamburg's Museum of Ethnology in Hamburg is widely considered to be one of the most important and in-depth collections of valuable ethnographic research in all of Europe.** With humble origins tracing back to 1849, the Museum of Ethnology has evolved significant over the last several decades, largely due to the efforts of Georg Thilenius, the full-time administrative director of the museum who assumed his position in 1904. Featuring a collection of over 350,000 valuable objects whose origins provide fascinating commentary on the people and culture of Germany and surrounding regions, a visit to the Museum of Ethnology is highly recommended for those who are eager to learn more about the origins of their country and the people who lived their before them. The museum is suitable for both adults and children.

Places To Eat

**Le Canard**

website: http://www.zarges-frankfurt.com/site/restaurant

*Our take:*

Very rarely do we have the opportunity to experience the degree of finesse and skill that head chef Ali Güngörmus wields when creating culinary offerings inspired by classic French cuisine, Mediterranean flair and Turkish exoticism. Although the ingredients may appear simple, rest assured that **Le Canard will provide you with a dining experience that is hard to find elsewhere in either the city or the world. This is truly a must-visit location in Hamburg.**

*Taken from the official website:*

"This is the literal translation of the Turkish surname of Güngörmüs. This optimistic energy can immediately be seen and tasted in the way Ali Güngörmüs creatively draws out and develops the innate qualities of the basic products he uses in his cuisine. At times Mediterranean, at times Middle-Eastern, with an air of the "1001 Nights". A happy liaison is achieved where the spices and aromas chosen subtly emphasize the character of the dish's basic products. "The best out of the simple" runs the ambitious motto of our committed chef de cuisine."
**Cuisine: French - Mediterranean Fusion**

**Landhaus Scherrer**

website: http://www.zarges-frankfurt.com/site/restaurant

*Our take:*

Having received a variety of honors and awards, including a much-coveted Michelin star, Landhaus Scherrer believes firmly that a winning recipe should be delivered to customers as often as possible. **The timeless collection of haute cuisine and continental masterpieces found here is sure to delight each of our inner gourmands**. For those who are interested in immersing themselves in fancy food and equally fancy company, Landhaus Scherrer is a must-visit location.

*Taken from the official website:*

"For more than 30 years the Landhaus Scherrer has settled itself among Hamburg's leading restaurants. The exclusive, Michelin-star honored haute cuisine, is incomparable and the favorite place to be for the lovers of fine food, as well as for the high society. The exclusive wine card is the perfect addition for a fully pleasured visit."
**Cuisine: Classic continental, luxury dining**

**Restaurant Engel**

website: http://www.restaurant-engel.de/index.php?id=restaurant

*Our take:*

Restaurant Engel is quite unique among the offerings found here, if only due to its beautiful location and outstanding culinary offerings. **Oluf Redlefsen and Christian Rach have teamed up to create a stand-out dining experience for those who may have grown tired of more traditional offerings in Hamburg and a looking for a scenic dining getaway that truly stands out from its competitors.**

*Taken from the official website (approximate translation):*

"Since 1994, the Angel Rocks has been located on the River Elbe . Oluf Redlefsen has built the restaurant on the former observation deck here. .In the period from 1999 to November 2007 Christian Rach has also joined the Angel team. . "Angel with Heart " applies to our guests as for the entire team

. We do not rely on the unique ambience and its prominent location, but want our guests to share in the enthusiasm for our angel."

**Cuisine: Contemporary Continental**

**Restaurant Vlet**

website: http://www.vlet.de

*Our take:*

There's absolutely nothing wrong (or audacious) about creating new dishes which, ultimately, are designed to become new classics within the 21st century's canon of luxe savoir fare. At Restaurant Vlet, **one gets the sense that the offerings they are being served have been conceived, prepared and delivered by culinary visionaries,** individuals who have no qualms with bucking trends, staring tradition in the face and stating, "try a bit, you'll love it".

*Taken from the official website (approximate translation):*

"Nowhere else in Hamburg does time seem – at first glance – to have stood still more than in the historic warehouse district, the *Speicherstadt*. Yet behind red brick buildings and between the canals, narrow alleyways and countless bridges, life pulsates like in hardly any other district in the Hanseatic city. Here, within just a stone's throw of the HafenCity, history meets with cosmopolitanism, and the past with futuristic visions. This unique combination can also be found here in VLET* – both on the plates and in the design!"

**Cuisine: French - Contemporary Fusion**

Places To Stay

**25 Hours Hotel Hafencity**

website: http://www.25hours-hotels.com/en/hafencity/home/home.html

*Our take:*

Acknowledging the need for an unassuming, comfortable respite from the hustle and bustle of Hamburg's thriving downtown, **the owners of 25 Hours Hotel Hafencity have created a domestic oasis that blurs the line between guest quarters and a "home away from home"**. 25 Hours Hotel Hafencity is both reasonably priced and generous in the amenities offered to travelers. 25 Hours Hotel Hafencity is highly recommended for those who prefer their travel to occur at a slower tempo.

*Taken from the official website:*

"Designed as a home away from home, the cabins and all of the rooms at the 25hours Hotel Hamburg HafenCity are warm and cozy. Features and materials inspired by the harbor and shipbuilding are interpreted with tongue-in-cheek humor and held together with sailors' yarns: 25 seafarers from around the world tell real-life stories of dangerous voyages, romantic encounters, violent storms and painful farewells. Anecdotal accessories and objects refer to these adventures, which are told in full in each cabin's logbook."

**Perfect for : Adults, Children, Couples, Families**

**East**

Website: http://www.25hours-hotels.com/en/hafencity/home/home.html

*Our take:*

Unlike many of its predecessors, East places special emphasis on embracing all that is cutting edge and new within Hamburg's dynamic cultural environment. Featuring an outstanding array of tech-related and domestic amenities, **East is the perfect destination for travelers who are hoping to remain "plugged-in" during their travels abroad and are prepared to pay slightly higher prices to do so.** Regardless of its trendy feel, East is perfectly suitable for both adults and children alike.

*Taken from the official website:*

"The design hotel east Hamburg has 128 rooms in various categories and sizes, ranging from 20m² to 50m². The sleek clarity of the rooms in east Hamburg is defined by the soothing lightness of the freestanding beds, the functionality of the technical fittings, the shimmering matt glass of the bathroom façade. Each room features a king-size bed, free W-LAN, air-conditioning, Sky entertainment TV, an iPod docking station, minibar, safe and desk. Every stay at the east Hotel in St. Pauli is an unforgettable experience!"

**Perfect for : Adults, Children, Couples, Families**

**Gastwerk Hotel Hamburg**

website: http://www.gastwerk.com

*Our take:*

Hamburg's Gastwerk Hotel prides itself on the distinctive flair found throughout the domestic quarters located here. **This "design hotel" is unique in that it has been purposefully crafted to created an ambience of unassuming comfort that will seduce all travelers who step foot inside**. The Gastwerk Hotel Hamburg has become incredibly popular in recent years, and remains on the preferred lists of many travelers who visit this area on a regular basis.

*Taken from the official website:*

"Is this really a hotel? Or could it be a lovingly furnished loft, the kind that reflects the distinctive individuality of good friends? Actually, both are true. At Hamburg's first Design Hotel you'll be greeted by the warmth and tranquil expanse of a painstakingly renovated historical brick building. Here in this former gasworks, you'll find the sort of genial hospitality that goes far beyond mere customer service. Come and make a new friend. The Gastwerk looks forward to your visit!"

**Perfect for : Adults, Children, Couples, Families**

**Side**

website: http://www.side-hamburg.de/side-home.html

*Our take:*

Yet another "design hotel", Side is located amongst Hamburg's diverse, eclectic and plentiful shopping arcades, all of which feature an array of products and services reflective of the unique cultural heritage of this area. **Featuring a visionary design and a beautiful lounge that has become the talk of the town amongst socialites and others, Side has quickly become a fixture in Hamburg's hospitality arena.** It is likely that, with time, this hotel will continue to attract new customers as well as retain an increasingly loyal customer base.

*Taken from the official website:*

"The one and only SIDE Hotel is the first and sole 5 star Design Hotel in Hamburg. Located near the inner Alster lake and the city's shopping arcades, it combines wellness with lifestyle and luxury with design. 11 floors of pure design composed by architect Matteo Thun lay between the spacious SPA-area and the impressive sky lounge. Discover the essence of indulgence in the restaurant [m]eatery where our chef prepares specialties meat. We bid you a warm welcome inSIDE."

**Perfect for : Adults, Children, Couples, Families**

**The George**

Website: https://www.thegeorge-hotel.de/in-hamburg/

*Our take:*

There's no shortage of anglophiles in Europe and abroad, and **The George is an excellent example of what could happen when a love of the monarchy is translated into a German hotel**. The George's unique decor is inspired by all things Britain, complete with flags, ornamental statues, etc. If you're looking for a unique hotel experience that will serve as a teleportation device of sorts, The George is for you!

*Taken from the official website:*

"British tradition with a touch of the modern and intercultural influences from colonial times. Located where Hamburg's colorful St. Georg district meets the Außenalster recreational area, The George Hotel Hamburg welcomes you with understated elegance, the DaCaio Restaurant with Italian cordiality and the in-house day spa with deep relaxation and renewed energy."

**Perfect for : Adults, Children, Couples, Families**

# Chapter 8
## Major Cities You Can't Miss - Munich

### Cultural Institutions - Museums

**Deutsches Museum**

Museumsinsel 1, 80538

München, Germany

Website: www.deutsches-museum.de/en

**The Deutsches Museum is the largest collection of science and technology-related exhibits in all of Germany.** First established in 1925, the museum now hosts well over 1.5 million visitors per year. The permanent collection at the Deutsches Museum currently holds over 28,000 objects from nearly 50 unique scientific and technological disciplines. The diverse array of objects on display here makes this particular museum ideal for young children. Adults will also enjoy the opportunity to critically examine a variety of objects that have revolutionized the way we live our lives. The museum is typically open throughout the year.

**BWM Museum**

Am Olympiapark 2, 80809

München, Germany

Website: http://www.bmw-welt.com/en/

Anyway who knows anything about automobiles or automotive history is probably well aware of just how large an impact that Germany has made on automotive culture. **The BMW Museum acts as a fascinating monument to the efforts and achievements of one of Germany's most popular automobile manufacturers.** First opened in 1973, the BMW Museum hosts well over 250,000 visitors on annual basis, many of whom are drawn here by the opportunity to gain an up close and personal look at both the manufacturing process for the BMW automobiles as well as the beautiful cars themselves. The museum features a "reverse spiral" design conceived of by Karl Schwanzer that draws inspiration from Frank Lloyd Wright's design of the Guggenheim Museum in New York City. The museum is commonly open throughout the year, barring holidays and designated closures. The BMW museum is ideal for adults, families and children.

Places To Eat

**Mark's**

Website: http://www.mandarinoriental.com/munich/fine-dining/restaurant-marks/

*Our take:*

If you're looking for luxury, then you've definitely come to the right place. Located within the world famous Mandarin Oriental hotel, Mark's has received recommendations from both the general public as well as the prestigious Michelin rating system. **With cuisine that reflects both refined French sensibilities and the exoticism of Asia, those who dine at Mark's will have the opportunity to partake in a sophisticated culinary fusion that will not disappoint.** Mark's also boasts one of the most impressive wine collections of any restaurant in the city. For those interested in experiencing the perfect pairing, the in-house sommelier is likely to have a number of recommendations available.

*Taken from the official website:*

"Offering one of the finest dining experiences in the city, one-Michelin starred Restaurant Mark's is one of Munich's most celebrated restaurants. Entered via a sweeping marble staircase leading up from the lobby, the elegant dining room enjoys an abundance of light provided by a combination of expansive windows and atmospheric lighting. With tables elegantly laid with white linen, the atmosphere is one of relaxed formality, suited to special occasions, business lunches and romantic dinners. In the evenings piano music drifts up from the lobby, creating a delightful ambience for our diners to enjoy. Showcasing Executive Chef Simon Larese's modern French cuisine, Restaurant Mark's serves a menu of classic French dishes inspired by the

delicious flavors of Asia. Using fresh, seasonal produce with ingredients brought in from Brittany and Normandy, the cuisine is sublime. We also boast a fantastic wine cellar housing over 300 exclusive vintages."
**Cuisine: French - Upscale French, Asian, Luxe Fusion**

**Tantris**

Website: http://www.tantris.de/restaurant_en.php

*Our take:*

In a marked departure from more conventional eateries in Munich, Tantris offers diners an otherworldly experience thanks to ravishing cuisine and one of the most atmospheric and unique restaurant interiors found anywhere in the city. Tantris makes no effort to conceal its marked departure from culinary norms. **Diners will be taken on a journey to parts unknown, with the only real guarantee being a meal that won't be forgotten for months to come.** This restaurant is highly recommended for individuals interested in experiencing some of the best contemporary cuisine that the city has to offer.

*Taken from the official website:*

"Welcome to the Main Room, where large-scale designs completed by the famous architect Justus Dahinden await. With its walls arching steeply to the centre of the room and wide glazed façades, this room is much loved for its dimensions, light and airiness. A warmth of colors, the materials used and the sincerity of service are all equally prevalent in this room."
**Cuisine: French - Trendy Contemporary**

**Atelier**

website: http://www.tantris.de/restaurant_en.php

*Our take:*

Adopting a seasonal and sustainable perspective on classic French cuisine, Atelier is rapidly becoming one of the most talked about restaurant in Munich. Thanks to the experience and talents of Atelier's head chef, and the extensive wine list on hand, those who decide to spend their evening at Atelier will likely enjoy themselves beyond what they thought was possible in the restaurant setting. **Atelier, while slightly pricey, is an undeniable fixture within Munich's restaurant scene that should be visited by any traveler with at least a passing interest in fine dining.**

*Taken from the official website:*

"If high cuisine alludes only to indulgence of the palate, we are happy to admit: this wouldn't satisfy us. Thus we designed a characteristic atmosphere, impressive yet at the same time inviting. Created by the Belgian art dealer Axel Vervoordt being at our Atelier makes you part of an impressive "Gesamtkunstwerk", an encounter of fine arts. At the intimate restaurant featuring 17 Gault Millau points, you will be captivated by the creative, seasonal gourmet cuisine from the chef Jan Hartwig. Enrico Spannenkrebs and his team delight you with first-class service and excellent wines. Discover the snug Privé or a small terrace sheltered by Amur maple trees - the Silent Garden. Your palate will be delighted. But your other senses will be as well."

**Cuisine: French - Sustainable, seasonal French**

Places To Stay

**The Cortiina Hotel**

Website: http://www.cortiina.com/rooms-and-rates.html

*Our take:*

With a decor that is reminiscent of the most luxurious of golden-era European resorts, the Cortiina Hotel has spared no expense when developing an ambience that will beguile all who step foot in its lobby area. The designers of the Cortiina Hotel have worked diligently to develop both an interior and exterior facade that draws inspiration from and use locally sourced building materials. With competitive pricing and an outstanding accommodation experience, **the Cortiina hotel is highly recommended for all who value on handcrafted, meticulously planned luxury and craftsmanship.**

*Taken from the official website:*

"Real beauty is in the details. Natural stone tiling in our bathrooms. Fresh flowers in every room. Dark oak furnishings, creating a feeling of wellbeing. After all, appearances count. A good night's rest for you is a top priority for us. You'll wake up refreshed after sleeping on a pure natural rubber mattress fitted with unbleached cotton sheets. For the recently finalized part of our hotel with a private entrance, local stone pine has mainly been chosen for the furniture."

**Perfect for : Adults, Children, Couples, Families**

**Eden Hotel Wolff**

Website: http://www.eden-hotel-wolff.de/english/

*Our take:*

Conventional luxury is, by no means, falling out of style. **The Eden Hotel Wolff has provided Munich with a truly outstanding institution which prides itself on delivering exceptional comfort and opulence to travelers hoping to stay here.** Thanks to a relatively advantageous positioning within close proximity to many of the cities most popular attractions, the Eden Hotel Wolff functions as a perfect "point-of-departure" for those who are hoping to enjoy a walking tour of the city that can also end with a beverage and savory meal at their hotel.

*Taken from the official website:*

"Since its founding in 1890 the traditional First Class Hotel is one of the leading names in Munich. The central location of our First Class Hotel opposite the central station with connection to all means of public transportation and the shuttle bus from and to the airport makes it a perfect starting point for our guests and their visit of Munich. Munich city and the pedestrian area starting at Karlsplatz/Stachus is within a short walking distance and leads to the most important sights of the historical Munich. Business trip, conference or short holiday - we are looking forward to welcome you at the Eden Hotel Wolff!."

**Perfect for : Adults, Children, Couples, Families**

**Mandarin Oriental Hotel Munich**

website: http://www.eden-hotel-wolff.de/english/

*Our take:*

By and large one of them most stand-out hotels in the entire country, the Mandarin Oriental Hotel Munich has transcended definitions of conventional luxury and entered a class all of its own. Featuring decor that is at once both sublimely beautiful and unassuming, the Mandarin Oriental Hotel Munich believes that luxury is as much a display of opulence as it is a feeling you get when you slip into bed at night. **Whether this is your first time staying at a Mandarin Oriental Hotel or one of several trips you have made to this particular institution, it is likely that it won't be your last!**

*Taken from the official website:*

"Tucked away in a quiet side street, Mandarin Oriental, Munich offers an enticing blend of luxury, comfort and style. Surrounded by some of the city's most famous sites, our hotel exudes a sense of elegant charm with a refined décor, beautiful roof-top pool, excellent restaurants and impeccable service."

**Perfect for : Adults, Children, Couples, Families**

**Hotel Jedermann**

Website:    http://www.hotel-jedermann.de/cms/index.php/en/hotel/history

*Our take:*

The story of the Hotel Jedermann is, by all accounts, a family affair. First acquired by Wener and Liselotte Jenke in 1961, the hotel has undergone an extensive series of renovations at the hands of this loving and dedicated family, each member of which has dedicated time and energy to ensuring that the Jedermann Hotel reaches its full potential. **Today, the hotel remains a fixture in Munich and is frequented by travelers from around the world**

**on a regular basis.** If you're looking for a hotel experience that leaves you feeling as if you've become part of a larger family or community, the Hotel Jedermann is highly recommended.

*Taken from the official website:*

"In 1961, the Hotel Jedermann was acquired by Werner and Liselotte Jenke. Through the years it was lovingly restored and enlarged with the help of the entire family. A big milestone were the Olympic Games in 1972. Several medal winners stayed in our hotel. In 1988 the Hotel Isaria next door was annexed to Hotel Jedermann and construction works began to improve the hotels standards. In 1995 we were one of the first hotels with its own homepage. Of course e-mail bookings and reservations were possible back then already. 2001 - the Jedermann celebrated its 40th anniversary with the total renovation of 14 rooms in 2002, some of them equipped with air conditioning."

**Perfect for : Adults, Children, Couples, Families**

**Hotel Torbräu**

Website: http://www.torbraeu.de/en/13hhista.php

*Our take:*

The Hotel Torbräu has an extensive history that spans a variety of formative events in Germany history. **For those seeking an opportunity to immerse themselves in an iconic fixture of German culture, the Hotel Torbräu is highly recommended.** Featuring an outstanding onsite restaurant and a modest yet refined decor in each of the rooms located here, the Hotel Torbräu provides guests within the opportunity to fully experience just how wonderful an evening in Munich can be

*Taken from the official website:*

"Completed around the turn of the millennium, the most significant structural and organizational changes since the rebuilding took place under Werner Kirchlechner, the sole general manager since **1993**: A completely reconfigured front desk and reception area, newly designed meeting facilities, a thorough overhaul of the CAFE AM ISARTOR and an elaborate renovation of the restaurant, giving it a Mediterranean theme. Each of the 91 tastefully appointed guest rooms is equipped with central heat and air as well as state-of-the art security and communication technology."

Perfect for : Adults, Children, Couples, Families

# Chapter 9
## Major Cities You Can't Miss- Cologne

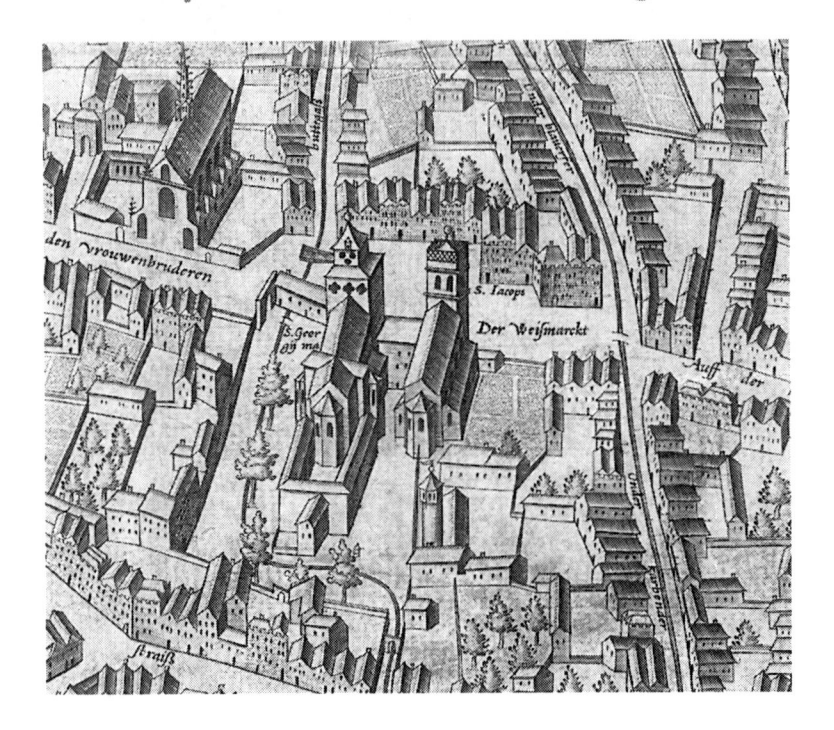

Cultural Institutions - Museums

**Museum Ludwig**

Heinrich-Böll-Platz, 50667

Köln, Germany

Website: www.**museum-ludwig**.de/en/

The Museum Ludwig houses one of the largest collection of contemporary and modern art in Cologne. Specific genres represented here include Surrealism, Abstract art, Pop Art, and others. Widely considered to be one of the largest collection of Picasso's art in Europe, the Museum Ludwig has also gained distinction for works form Andy Warhol and Roy Lichtenstein. Museum Ludwig first emerged as an independent entity in Cologne in 1976. **Not only does the museum host a vast collection of acclaimed visual art, but it is also home to the Cologne Philharmonic, the city's acclaimed**

**symphonic ensemble.** The museum presents the annual "Wolfgang Hahn Prize" to an international artist who has been selected by jury. The museum's collection is suitable for both adults and children alike. Museum Ludwig is typically open throughout the year, barring holidays and scheduled closures.

Places To Eat

**4 Cani**

Website: http://www.4cani.com/en/cani/mood.php

*Our take:*

Featuring what is arguably one of the most welcoming and receptive environments of any restaurant in Cologne, 4 Cani has developed a loyal following of both locals and tourists alike. Featuring a menu that spans the gamut from eclectic continental to Mediterranean, **4 Cani has fast become a fixture in an otherwise competitive restaurant environment in Cologne.** For those who have yet to dine here before or are visiting the city for the first time, a trip to 4 Cani will serve as an excellent introduction to local culture and a strong indication of how unique this city really is.

*Taken from the official website:*

"The doors of the 4 Cani are always open for you. Here you can meet people you like. Enjoy our healthy products of high quality and treat yourself with fine food, served by our friendly service staff. You can get all this for a fair price which enables you visit the Cani on a regular basis. Our kitchen freshly prepares the well-known "ingenious Cani food". Our guests are nice and open-minded people. You are served by friendly and qualified staff. Experience the "Cani Mood". A fresh Italian crossover cuisine with genuine roots. Good products, creativity and quality are the basis for the 4 Cani food which has a wide horizon towards Asia and the Pacific. Authentic creations of our international team of chefs provides the particular enjoyable gustatory experience."

**Cuisine: French - Casual, Continental, Mediterranean Fusion**

**Restaurant Vendôme**

Website: http://www.schlossbensberg.com/en

*Our take:*

The Restaurant Vendôme has proven itself to be one of Cologne's most sought after culinary destinations. **Thanks to a menu that has entranced the population of this beautiful city, this particular restaurants is heavily trafficked by both tourists and locals alike.** Those hoping for a table at Restaurant Vendôme are advised to place their reservations well in advance, as the experience here is one of the most highly prized in the city at large. !

Featuring a reputation that far precedes any visit to the restaurant itself, the Restaurant Vendôme is widely considered to be one of the most luxurious restaurants in the entirety of Cologne. Having been awarded multiple Michelin Stars, this particularly culinary institution could easily be content to rest on its laurels. That being said, head chef Joachim Wissler continues to refine his craft and ensure that those who dine here are constantly reminded of just how sublime a properly prepared meal can be. Those who are interested in dining at Restaurant Vendome are advised to make reservations well in advance, as this particular institution is quite popular among tourists and locals alike.

*Taken from the official website:*

"The restaurant Vendôme, near Cologne, headed by 3-star chef Joachim Wissler, is one of the best restaurants in Germany. Joachim Wissler serves a blend of classical cuisine, creativity and modernity. In 2005 and 2013, the magazine "Der Feinschmecker" voted Wissler "Chef of the Year" and in 2009 he was deemed "The Best Chef in Germany. Apart from three Michelin stars, the restaurant Vendôme has also been decorated with 19.5 Gault Millau points as well as 5 Feinschmecker F's, and is ranked 12th in the "San Pellegrino World's 50 Best Restaurants 2014" list.."

**Cuisine: French, Classic continental**

**Restaurant Lerbach**

Website: http://www.schlossbensberg.com/en

*Our take:*

The culinary offerings at Restaurant Lerbach easily stand out from the crowd, due in large part to the talents of Nils Henkel, **a chef who understands how important subtlety and grace are when preparing meals with flavor profiles designed to withstand the test of time.** At Restaurant Lerbach, it's easy to get lost in the myriad of culinary delights featuring outstanding produce and growers from the region. Restaurant Lerbach offers their local ecology a degree of respect and care which help to ensure that all meals taken here are absolutely delicious. Highly recommended.

*Taken from the official website:*

"With lightness and transparency 2-star chef Nils Henkel has developed a gourmet cuisine that is absolutely unique. He manages to create pure freshness, condensed aromas and novel textures for menus that succeed in astounding his guests again and again. Particularly the herbs give his aroma cuisine that special something. Care and respect for nature are the foundation of his culinary art. That is why he only uses ingredients from the local region and from producers who he keeps in touch with personally. This is by no means a backwards-looking mindset. In fact, concentrating on the true values, especially in the kitchen, makes good sense in terms of sustainability and in this case tastes absolutely delicious.."

**Cuisine: Sustainable gourmet**

**Heising and Adelmann**

Website: http://www.schlossbensberg.com/en

*Our take:*

Thanks to a friendly, welcoming atmosphere and dual restaurant / bar environment, **Heising and Adelmann will serve as an excellent destination for both formal dinners and a casual night out on the town.** Although many tourists traveling through Cologne get caught up in the ritz and glamour of many of the more luxe restaurants in town, Heising and Adelmann is a fantastic gem that is guaranteed to impress all who decide to take a chance on it. A must-visit location for travelers interesting in exploring available culinary options which are off the beaten path.

*Taken from the official website:*

"For over ten years, Heising & Adelmann has functioned as a unique combination of restaurant and bar, combining excellent food with an unbeatable atmosphere . We are pleased to welcome you into our house, which is centrally located in the heart of the cathedral city of Cologne , welcome .

**Cuisine: Classic, upscale**

Places To Stay

**Hyatt Regency Cologne**

Website: http://cologne.regency.hyatt.com/en/hotel/home.html

*Our take:*

Although some may be quick to write off an international hotel chain during their trip to some of Europe's more unique destinations, the **Hyatt Regency Cologne has been designed with a level of attention to detail which ensures that even the most discerning of travelers will find something here that delights and entertains them.** One of the more resplendent hotels in Cologne, the Hyatt Regency successfully merges old-world charm with new-world delights that are guaranteed to satisfy all who visit. Relatively reasonable prices also ensure that visitors can stay here without breaking the bank.

*Taken from the official website:*

"Hyatt Regency Cologne is a luxury hotel located in the city centre of Cologne, Germany - on the right bank of the River Rhine in Deutz. Cologne Cathedral (Kölner Dom), the Lanxess Arena (former Koelnarena) event hall and the Koelnmesse trade fair and exhibition centre are within walking distance. The spacious and modern rooms and suites offer spectacular views over the River Rhine, the Old Town and the world-famous Cologne Cathedral. Our luxury hotel is just a 15-minute drive away from Cologne/Bonn Airport."

**Perfect for : Adults, Children, Couples, Families**

**Excelsior Hotel Ernst**

Website:    http://www.excelsiorhotelernst.com/en/the-hotel.html

*Our take:*

One of many hotels throughout Cologne that prides itself on exceptional service and equally impressive atmosphere, the **Excelsior Hotel Ernst may be the perfect location for those who are passionate about indulging in a top-flight hotel experience during their stay in the city.** Prices here reflect the high level of attention placed upon the offered amenities. While this hotel certainly isn't for everyone, it is highly recommended for travelers who have no qualms with enjoying all that Cologne has to offer.

*Taken from the official website*

"The Excelsior Hotel Ernst is Cologne's Grand Hotel next to the Cathedral. We provide individualized services to respond to the uniqueness of every guest and employee. We maintain the tradition of hospitality and remain modern by applying innovation. As Grand Hotel in the heart of Cologne, we actively participate in urban life and we are committed to art and culture. Your individuality is our excellence.."

**Perfect for : Adults, Children, Couples, Families**

**Schlossshotel Lenbach**

Website:    http://www.schlosshotel-lerbach.com/en/discover-the-hotel

*Taken from the official website:*

"Althoff Schlosshotel Lerbach in Bergisch Gladbach near to Cologne is considered as one of the best luxury hotels in Germany. It provides a perfect setting for any occasion; for an epicurean fling, an exhilarating celebration, or a romantic weekend for two. You will sense at your arrival just what an extraordinary place the castle hotel is - this enchanting hotel, with its imposing facade entwined in vines, is situated in the middle of an enormous private park."

**Perfect for : Adults, Children, Couples, Families**

**Dorint Am Heumark Koeln**

Website:   http://www.fivestaralliance.com/4star-hotels/cologne/dorint-am-heumarkt-koeln

*Taken from the official website:*

Enjoy Luxury at the Dorint Am Heumarkt Koeln- one of the best business hotels in Cologne! The hotel is situated in a prime location of the city centre only a few steps away from the old town, the Cologne Cathedral, shopping miles and further attractions like the fair grounds. The hotel incorporates a unique combination of modern design and historical elements. The 250 luxurious rooms and 12 suites offer highest lifestyle and modern technological equipment including air conditioning, three phones, pay-tv, modem plug as well as broadband internet access, an in room safe and coffee and tea making facilities The unique lifestyle of the Dorint Am Heumarkt Koeln is also reflected in the restaurants "Maulbeers" and "Faveo" , in the trendy "Harry's New-York Bar" , in the wine room "Vecino" and in the historical fire place room "Overstolz".

**Perfect for : Adults, Children, Couples, Families**

**Pullman Hotels**

Website:   http://www.pullmanhotels.com/gb/discovering-pullman-hotel/pullman-in-motion.shtml

*Taken from the official website:*

"Work Hard, Play Hard. Pullman hotels cultivate the art of enjoying those moments when work stops and leisure begins. Swimming pool, spa, Fit

Lounge – comfortable, beautifully designed spaces where a business traveler can put business aside. For a moment.".

Perfect for : Adults, Children, Couples, Families

# Chapter 10
## Major Cities You Can't Miss- Stuttgart

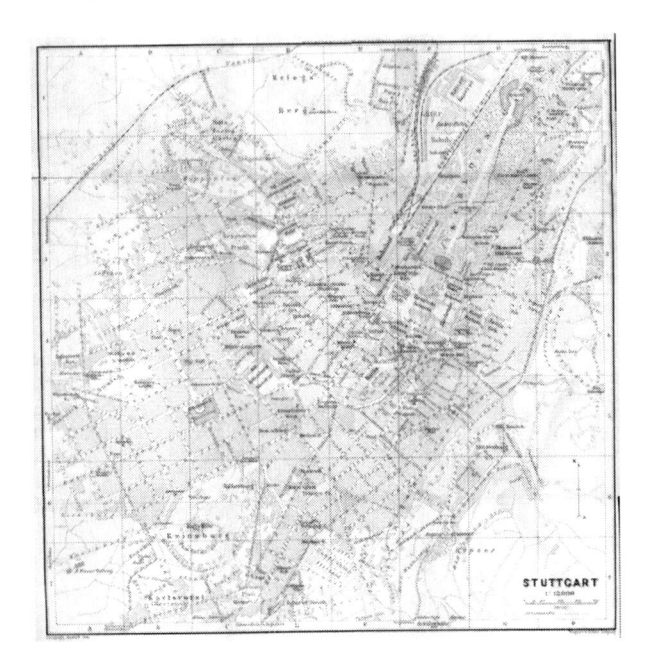

Cultural Institutions - Museums

**Staatsgalerie Stuttgart**

Konrad-Adenauer-Straße 30-32,

D-70173 Stuttgart, Germany

Website: http://www.staatsgalerie.de/museum_e

Considered to be one of the more trafficked museums in Stuttgart and the country at large, the Staatsgalerie Stuttgart offers visitors the opportunity to browse a permanent collection of nearly 800 paintings, prints and photographs, as well as explore a multitude of traveling exhibitions that showcase the works of various creative talents from throughout Europe at large. The museum prides itself on launching between seven and eight major exhibitions on a yearly basis here. The Staatsgalerie Stuttgart is suitable for both adults and children. The museum is typically open throughout the year, with various closings occurring on national holidays and stated closure days.

Places To Eat

## Cube

Website: http://cube-restaurant.de

*Taken from the official website (approximate translation):*

"The sense of space is unique , glass on all sides and a fantastic view of Stuttgart center . The reduced interior design veteran Heinz Witthöft supports the impression of urban generosity . The professional restaurant crew has a clear vision : " deliver a new dining experience! " This is a commitment in this outstanding setting."

**Cuisine: Classic, luxe**

## Olivo

website: http://www.olivo-restaurant.de/en/Philosophy

*Taken from the official website:*

"The gourmet restaurant OLIVO under the direction of Michelin-starred chef Nico Burkhardt conjures culinary pleasure on the highest level. The amazing, delicate creations are inspired by French cuisine and interpreted in a modern way. Burkhardt's style is light and sophisticated. his aim is to offer his guests the best flavors and absolute pleasure. To do this he plays with textures and celebrates his perfectionism. Our sommelier will recommend carefully selected wines from our cellar while you dine undisturbed in OLIVO's modern and stylish atmosphere."
**Cuisine: French - French, classic / contemporary**

## Amadeus

Website: http://www.olivo-restaurant.de/en/Philosophy

*Our take:*

At Amadeus, it's easy to understand why so many people consider this particular dining establishment to be the best possible location for a night out on the town with friends and family. **Thanks to an affordable and high-quality wine and beer selection, the delicious meals offered here have the perfect pairing on hand.** Amadeus is highly recommended for those who are searching for an affordable dining option in Stuttgart that will easily satisfy a variety of palates.

*Taken from the official website*

"A very special ambience in the old orphanage . Here you will find for any occasion your personal favorite place - in the cozy corner for two, to dinner with friends at the big table or a hearty beer or a good wine at a lively bar We spoil you with always fresh , large and small . courts . Schwäbisch and yet a bit more!."
Cuisine: French - Mediterranean Fusion

## Délice

Website: http://www.restaurant-delice.de/01_gastrosophie_englisch/f_gastrosophie_e.html

*Taken from the official website*

"It is our desire to spoil our guests' senses with harmony, love and creativity. We would like to invite you to experience leisurely selected dishes with exclusive and tasteful, complementing wines from our wine cellar. Naturally all dishes are prepared fresh and created to suit the particular season. Specially selected ingredients, delivered by our faithful suppliers, are a part of this exceptionally tasteful experience. We primarily use local victuals. First and foremost the decision is for a healthy quality, but also for the better and more authentic taste, because only the authentic taste is consistent with our idea of 'gastrosophy'. Really quite simple..."
Cuisine: French - Mediterranean Fusion

Places To Stay

## Dormero Hotel Stuttgart

Website: http://http://www.dormero-hotel-stuttgart.de/en/

*Taken from the official website:*

"**DORMERO Hotel Stuttgart** welcomes you in an environment of modern design and outstanding comfort, right in the center of an enticing leisure center. Several restaurants, modern bars and pubs, two musical venues, the Stuttgart casino, a CinemaxX theater and the unique 'SchwabenQuellen' wellness center offer you near endless opportunities to enjoy your stay in Stuttgart. With a total of 454 rooms and suites in two towers (Red Wing and White Wing), *DORMERO Hotel Stuttgart* is fully integrated in Stuttgart's SI-Centrum. All rooms offer the highest standards of sleeping comfort supported with the newest amenities in a laidback and relaxed atmosphere.."

**Perfect for : Adults, Children, Couples, Families**

**Pullman Stuttgart Fontana**

Website: http://http://www.dormero-hotel-stuttgart.de/en/

*Taken from the official website:*

"The stylish Hotel Pullman Stuttgart Fontana is popular with discerning business travelers. The new exhibition center is as easy to get to from here as Stuttgart's musical venues, and the adjacent park has green space for you to stroll through. Here for meetings? The hotel offers nine conference rooms and all you need to get work done comfortably and effectively."

**Perfect for : Adults, Children, Couples, Families**

**Hotel Am Schlossgarten**

website: http://http://www.dormero-hotel-stuttgart.de/en/

*Taken from the official website:*

"This international 5-star hotel is situated in the park landscape of the castle gardens of Stuttgart closest proximity to the Königstraße shopping area as well as many cultural institutions such as the city theatre, the famous ballet and opera house, the city gallery, and the new as well as the old castle and belongs to The Leading Hotels of the World®. The luxurious hotel is only a few minutes away on foot from the central train station Stuttgart.."

**Perfect for : Adults, Children, Couples, Families**

**City Hotel Stuttgart**

Website: http://cityhotel-stuttgart.de/index.php?lang=en_&selItem=aufenthalt

*Taken from the official website:*

"Our little refurbished hotel offers our guests a comfortable and personal atmosphere in the heart of the city of Stuttgart and is therefore an ideal starting point for business and private related activities.

All rooms are friendly and modern arranged."

**Perfect for : Adults, Children, Couples, Families**

**Mercure Hotel Stuttgart City Center**

Website: http://cityhotel-stuttgart.de/index.php?lang=en_&selItem=aufenthalt

*Taken from the official website:*

"If you value a central location, the 3-star Superior Mercure Hotel Stuttgart City Center is the ideal choice for you. All 174 rooms have air conditioning and free WIFI. Our meeting area includes six rooms that can be combined to hold up to 200 people, who have easy access to the hotel by train, as the main train station is 875 yards away. The nearest highway is the A81, just 1.2 miles away, while the airport and exhibition center are 9.3 miles away. You can park your car in our underground car park."

**Perfect for : Adults, Children, Couples, Families**

**Park Inn By Radisson**

Website: http://cityhotel-stuttgart.de/index.php?lang=en_&selItem=aufenthalt

*Taken from the official website:*

"Enviably located in the city centre, this sleek hotel houses Stuttgart visitors in style. Guests are only 200 meters from the bustling plaza, Marienplatz, and public transport is easily accessible. Corporate travelers can reach key business sites like the Porsche headquarters and Daimler AG. Appealing to sightseers as well, the hotel's position in Stuttgart is also convenient to museums and theatres. In addition to 181 well-appointed guest rooms, the Park Inn features an on-site restaurant, modern fitness facilities and state-of-the-art meeting rooms."

**Perfect for : Adults, Children, Couples, Families**

# Chapter 11
# Major Cities You Can't Miss - Dresden

Cultural Institutions - Museums

**Staatsgalerie Stuttgart**

Taschenberg 2, 01067

Dresden, Germany

website: www.skd.museum

Dresden Castle currently holds the distinction of being one of the oldest buildings in the entirety of Dresden. This should not come as too much of a surprise, however, as much of the city was, unfortunately, destroyed during the Second World War. The Dresden Castle has served as the home of a variety of aristocratic individuals throughout the history of Germany, including multiple Kings of Saxony. Today, visitors have the opportunity to explore the castle itself as well as a museum which is housed onsite. The museum contains an extensive collection of prints, drawings, photographs, and an acclaimed art library. Tours of Dresden Castle are suitable for both adults and children alike. The castle is typically open throughout the year, although various closures may occur during national holidays.

Places To Eat

**Lesage**

website: http://www.lesage.de/#

*Taken from the official website (approximate translation):*

"A car factory in which olive oil is used for cooking? Chef Thorsten Bubolz doesn't find this unusual at all. He prepares delicious meals in the midst of an extraordinary setting, the former automobile factory for Gläserne VW"

Cuisine:

**Villandry**

website: http://www.villandry.de/restaurant.html

*Taken from the official website (approximate translation):*

"The restaurant Villandry we want to make it easy for you to escape the daily routine and embark on our whimsical delights ...Our kitchen offers the use of fresh and mostly local produce . Flavored with spices and side dishes from around the world will lead to simple but imaginative dishes that always have something in common : modern, light , Mediterranean ...The almost daily updated menu will be presented on a slate at the table and carefully selected wine list contains so many big names and places with new , young winemakers fresh accents . In the warmer months, we also serve our food in wonderful summer garden in the leafy , quiet backyard in the Dresden Neustadt ."

Cuisine:

**Alte Meister**

website: http://www.villandry.de/restaurant.html

*Taken from the official website (approximate translation):*

"The Alte Meister café & restaurant was opened in October 2001 on the premises of Albert Braun's former studio. Braun directed the artistic renovation of the Zwinger after World War II.In the museum café of the world-famous gallery of the same name, we now offer freshly made delicacies of creative international cuisine ."

Cuisine:

**Sophienkeller**

website: http://www.villandry.de/restaurant.html

*Taken from the official website (approximate translation):*

"You will find the restaurant in the historical centre of Dresden in the vaulted ceilings of the "Taschenbergpalais" opposite to the chimes pavilion of the "Dresdner Zwinger". On the outskirts and easy to reach by foot are the "Semperoper", the "Goldene Reiter", the "Brühlsche Terrasse" and the "Frauenkirche". Entering these historical vaults of the Taschenbergpalais opposite the Zwinger you step back into the 18th century, and enter the world of August the Strong. Let yourself feast on Saxon specialties served to you by lovely maidens. Wherever you look – in the Monastery Bakery with ist historic oven, the museum with ist impressive Table of Nobles, the large Build Hall or the small one, or the guardians passage – you will find fascinating evidence of a time long gone by. Some of the original walls of the "Einsiedelsche Häuser" buildings, dating back to the 14th century, can still be seen – in the place which was at the foundation of Saxony's Glory."

Cuisine:

Places To Stay

**Hotel Taschenbergpalais**

website: http://www.kempinski.com/en/dresden/hotel-taschenbergpalais/overview/

*Taken from the official website:*

"Built in the 18th century by the Saxon king, August "the Strong", as a pledge of love to his mistress and faithfully restored in 1995, the Grand Hotel Taschenbergpalais Kempinski is a beautiful combination of historic glory, contemporary elegance and modern design.

The hotel offers 182 elegant rooms, 32 luxurious suites and culinary excellence from five different venues including: the gourmet restaurant Intermezzo, the Palais Bistro serving French cuisine, the Restaurant Lesage in the Transparent Factory of Volkswagen, Café Vestibül with its own patisserie and the Karl May Bar with an award-winning cocktail list serving more than 100 different kinds of whiskies. There are six elegant conference rooms on the Bel Etage and a divisible meeting and ball room for up to 500 people.

The hotel has also its own spa lounge with a pool, wellness & beauty treatments and offers five-star catering services.

Perfect for : Adults, Children, Couples, Families

**Swissotel Dresden**

website: http://www.swissotel.com/hotels/dresden/

*Taken from the official website:*

"The exclusive hotel Swissotel Dresden Am Schloss is located in the heart of historic Old Town. Its central location, great shopping, entertainment and nearby historical sites such as the Semper Opera and Zwinger Palace make this the perfect gateway to the city's business and culture. Swissotel Dresden's historic facade houses stylishly modern interior design, with cutting-edge technology and the warmth of Swiss hospitality. 235 elegant rooms & suites are designed for comfort and style, with state-of-the-art technology and all the services and conveniences you need, such as a free internet connection. Innovative Swiss cuisine is the cornerstone of the hotel's Wohnstube restaurant, for quick & healthy snacks or elegant formal dining. A sumptuous breakfast buffet at Esszimmer offers a wide range of choices to energize your day."

Perfect for : Adults, Children, Couples, Families
**Pullman Dresden Newa**

website: www.pullman-hotel-dresden.de/

*Taken from the official website:*

"Near Dresden Central Station this exclusive 4-star Hotel Pullman Dresden Newa rises 14 floors high above Dresden's most popular shopping boulevard. The pleasant hotel's atmosphere upon Prager Strasse and the subtle classic room design offer pleasant rest and clarity. Floor to ceiling panoramic windows open a unique view to baroque Dresden skyline. In the restaurant Le Boulevard chef Dieter Dornig serves demanding Saxon cuisine. For peace and tranquility see the in-house Gingko Spa. For up to 300 people, Pullman Dresden Newa Hotel is a professional host for events and conference.."

Perfect for : Adults, Children, Couples, Families

**Hotel AM Terrassenufer**

website: www.hotel-terrassenufer.de/en/

*Taken from the official website:*

"The first class hotel "Am Terrassenufer" is situated near the historic part of the town in the inner city of Dresden. Its international character turns your stay into a relaxing experience not only for businessmen but also for holiday-makers. From the Bruehlsche Terrace near the hotel you can get a view of the "Florence on the Elbe" with its "White Fleet" and the famous skyline. All famous sights as well as the commercial center and the government sector can be reached on foot in a few minutes."

Perfect for : Adults, Children, Couples, Families

**Radisson Blu Park Hotel & Conference Center, Dresden**

website: http://www.radissonblu.com/parkhotel-dresdenradebeul/

*Taken from the official website:*

"Nestled in the hills of Germany's renowned wine region, the Radisson Blu Park Hotel offers Radebeul lodging in scenic surroundings. The Dresden city centre lies just a few kilometers from the accommodation, and the airport is a mere nine kilometers away."

**Perfect for : Adults, Children, Couples, Families**

# Chapter 12
## Major Cities You Can't Miss- Bremen

### Cultural Institutions - Museums

**Kunsthalle Bremen**

Am Wall 207, 28195

Bremen, Germany

website: www.kunsthalle-bremen.de/

The Kunsthalle Bremen is widely considered by local authorities to be one of the best locations in the city for those who would like to explore the fascination world of European classic and contemporary art. The collection includes artwork dating as far back as the 14th century and as recent as new media productions from the 21st century. The Department of Prints and Drawings at the Kunsthalle Bremen is widely considered to be the largest of its kind in all of Europe.

### Places To Stay

**Dorint Park Hotel**

website: http://hotel-bremen.dorint.com/en/

*Taken from the official website:*

"The city is 38 km long and 16 km wide. And in the middle of the city our Dorint Park Hotel Bremen is located in the green heart of the city - the public park "Am Bürgerpark". 175 stylish and comfortable rooms and suites have a beautiful view into the countryside. Relax in our 1,200 m² large Vitality Spa area, which is a true paradise for spa lovers. Whether heated outdoor pool, whirlpool, saunas and steam baths, snow grotto, relaxation area or solarium - everything is waiting for your relaxation. Furthermore, you can choose from a range of spa and cosmetic treatments in our beauty department!"

**Perfect for : Adults, Children, Couples, Families**

**Atlantic Grand Hotel Bremen**

website: www.atlantic-hotels.de/

*Taken from the official website:*

"The ATLANTIC Grand Hotel Bremen has made its mark on the hotel scene in the federal state of Bremen. Whether you are a business traveler, conference guest, or visitor to Bremen, you can reside and meet in a special setting in the heart of the historic part of town, between the market square, Boettcherstrasse, and the Schlachte promenade on the Weser river. Our establishment's interior design reflects the high standards that one expects of an innovative and modern hotel. The colors and furniture are perfectly matched and convey a feeling of comfort and coziness in your "home from home. First class through and through is the motto that the ATLANTIC hotels live by. Facilities that go without saying, such as Internet access for our hotel and conference guests, are provided by us free of charge."

Perfect for : Adults, Children, Couples, Families

**City Hotel**

website: http://hotel-bremen.dorint.com/en/

*Taken from the official website:*

"This hotel was renovated and modernized in 2003, including 39 rooms (of which 5 are suites) spread over 5 floors. Facilities on offer include a stylish foyer with a 24-hour reception desk and bar, express checkout and a lift. In addition, the hotel has installed a WLAN access point, which may be used by hotel guests.   City Hotel Bremen is located close to the main train station, the convention centers as well as the town hall and the congress centre. The famous town hall, the market place as well as the picturesque old town of Bremen are also only a few minutes away. Bremen airport is additionally only about 5 km away. There is a good tramway connection to the Weser Stadion for our football fans of Werder Bremen and guests."

**Perfect for:** Adults, Children, Couples, Families

## Conclusion
### Aren't You Excited? Your Journey Begins Now!

As you can see, there are no shortage of fascinating diversions in what is widely considered to be one of the most diverse and satisfying countries in Europe. As stated previously, we hope that you will be able to use this guide as a comprehensive survey of all that this wonderful land has to offer. There will, of course, be hundreds of entertaining attractions that we have forgotten to mention. This, however, also serves to highlight one of the most enjoyable elements of the travel experience: the element of surprise. No matter how well prepared you may feel regarding the list of destinations and attractions for your adventure, we guarantee that you will discover a host of opportunities to venture outside of your realm of knowledge or comfort and discover a wonderful world that defies imagination. There's never been a better time to embark upon an adventure to Germany. We hope you have a wonderful adventure!

Germany isn't the easiest place to understand. Even the Spanish themselves can't put their finger on why they're so, well, different. This guidebook doesn't pretend to know everything or offer the complete comprehension of this eclectic and eccentric nation. Anyone claiming to have the divine handbook on Germany has missed the point. You're not supposed to understand it. You're supposed to indulge and explore one of the planet's most surreal experiences. It's not supposed to make sense. Just smile and shake your head.

But while we're not offering the holy grail we like to think that this guidebook opens up Germany and ensures you can maximize the experience. It's a route planner, travel guide, and hand holder throughout. If it's not, then drop us a line and let us know what could have made it better.

There's an array of Germany guidebooks. You chose this one. So thank you. We mean that, it's not always easy to entice the reader away from regurgitated profit maximizers so many travel guides out there. Thank you for choosing a guidebook written by local experts. And thank you for reading. Many many hours (too many) went into this, and the writing wouldn't have a purpose if it wasn't for the reader. Wherever you're reading this…thank you again.

So it's goodbye from us. Although, let's remember, that the best thing about saying goodbye is that you can say hello again. So check out our other travel guides and hopefully our paths will cross once more. In the meantime, enjoy Germany and immerse yourself in the experience. It's a once in a lifetime journey, even if you've been before…

Enjoy your trip!

*Dagny Taggart*

## Learn German Before You Leave - 300% FASTER!

## \>\> Check Out The Most Awarded German Online Course In Existence (with Audio Lessons!) <<

Wouldn't it be great to learn German before your trip begins? Indeed, it would. Now, let me ask you: what if you could learn it extremely *fast*?

If you truly want to learn German 300% FASTER, then hear this out.

I've partnered with the most revolutionary language teachers to bring you the very best German online course I've ever seen. It's a mind-blowing program specifically created for language hackers such as ourselves. It will allow you learn German 3x faster, straight from the comfort of your own home, office, or wherever you may be. It's like having an unfair advantage!

**The Online Course consists of:**

+ 190 Built-In Lessons
+ 99 Interactive Audio Lessons
+ 24/7 Support to Keep You Going

The program is extremely engaging, fun, and easy-going. You won't even notice you are learning a complex foreign language from scratch. And before you realize it, by the time you go through all the lessons you will officially become a truly solid German speaker.

Old classrooms are a thing of the past. It's time for a language revolution.

If you'd like to go the extra mile follow the link below, and let the revolution begin!

\>\> http://www.bitly.com/German-Course <<

## CHECK OUT THE COURSE »

### PS: Can I Ask You a Quick Favor?

**If you liked the book, please leave a nice review on Amazon! I'd absolutely love to hear your feedback.** Every time I read your reviews... you make me smile. I'd be immensely thankful if you go to Amazon now, and write down a quick line sharing with me your experience. I personally read ALL the reviews there, and I'm thrilled to hear your feedback and honest motivation. It's what keeps me going, and helps me improve everyday =)

*Please go Amazon now and drop a quick review sharing your experience!*

\*\*\*

THANKS!

\*\*\*

ONCE YOU'RE BACK,
FLIP THE PAGE!
BONUS CHAPTER AHEAD
=)

# Preview Of "German For Tourists - The Most Essential German Guide to Travel Abroad, Meet People & Find Your Way Around - All While Speaking Perfect German!"

## Introduction

### Why should YOU learn German?

Looking to spend some time in Berlin, Germany's hip, buzzing capital? Or maybe you want to chat to the locals over some frothy beers at next year's Oktoberfest in Munich? Planning an important business meeting with German clients? Looking for new customers abroad? Dating a gorgeous German or planning a move to a German-speaking country?

Then this book is the right starting place for you!

Whether you have a little rusty German left over from your schooldays or whether you are a complete beginner, this book will give you a clear idea of what the German language is and how to use it. Instead of slaving away over grammar books for hours, we'll give you the tools that you need to start using your German quickly, so that you can get out there and enjoy speaking it.

German has something of a reputation as a difficult language to learn but that doesn't have to be the case. This book will make it fun and easy and will of course make the most of that famous German efficiently!

By the end of this course you will have will be able to experience the wonderful feeling that comes with being able to communicate and have fun in another language. YOU CAN DO IT! YOU CAN SPEAK GERMAN!

### How will YOU learn German in a few weeks?

When you see the German language for the first time it may seem very foreign indeed, using strange symbols and letters that we don't use in English, but as an English-speaker you already know a lot more German than you realize!

English and German both belong to the same family of languages, the 'West Germanic' group. Although both languages have since borrowed heavily from many other languages such as Latin, French and Greek, these German roots still remain and as you progress with your German you will begin to recognize more and more of them. Despite the different spellings, an English speaker will have no problem guessing the meanings of words such as 'Haus' (house), 'Kaffee' (coffee), 'Medizin' (medicine) or thousands more. You'll soon realize that a lot of vocabulary learning in German has already been done for you. Although the nature of German as a language means that it is very capable of creating new words to keep up with modern innovations, German has also adopted a great many loan words from modern English. It doesn't take much imagination to guess the meanings of verbs such as 'downloaden', 'skypen'or even 'ausflippen'(to flip out)!

In this course, basic grammar elements will be explained to you as we go to build up your understanding, but our focus is going to be on building up a vocabulary of commonly used words and phrases so that you can get out there as soon as possible and start SPEAKING German, which is the really fun part and the best way to keep on improving your language skills.

Let's now wait any longer but dive into our learning program….and most of all, ENJOY every step of the journey!

# Chapter 1
## Getting along in German with the Basics

What you're about to learn:
- An introduction to German language and culture
- A background to German tradition and customs
- How to pronounce German words
- How to build a sentence in German

German Culture and Civilization

### Countries where German is spoken

German and variations of it is spoken by around 120 million people worldwide. It is the official language of Germany, Austria and Liechtenstein and one of the official languages of Switzerland, Luxembourg and Belgium, as well as being spoken as a minor language in other countries such as Italy, Slovenia, Hungary and Poland as well as in Namibia (as a result of colonialism) and in some South American countries due to German emigration. As well as the official language *Hochdeutsch* or 'Standard German' which is the equivalent of Oxford English, some countries have their own standardized variants such as 'Austrian German' and 'Swiss Standard German'.

### A Snapshot of German Culture

German culture began long before the birth of Germany as unified nation state in 1871 and spanned the entire German-speaking world from the North Sea to the Balkans. Historically Germany has been called *Das Land der Dichter und Denker* or 'the country of poets and thinkers'. It was the threads of a common German language and a shared Literature dating back from the Middle Ages and including Goethe, Schiller, Mann and Hesse, shared philosophy from Leibnitz and Kant to Nietzsche and a shared musical culture taking in Bach, Beethoven, Wagner, Liszt and Mahler that drew the country together.

Germany is a country of both similarities and differences. The many lands brought together to form Modern Germany are very varied in their culture and dialects. There are many differences between the Frisians living on the lowlands of northern Germany, the stoic Prussians of the east and the conservative Bavarians. Local characters, accents and dialects are as varied as the landscape.

The young German nation, having only been unified in 1871 was to be divided again following the Second World War, this time into East and West. For over 40 years the Deutsche Demokratische Republik or East Germany kept behind the Iron Curtain and was isolated from the Western German states. This division left a legacy with the eastern states and years after reunification the east of the country is still working to catch up with the prosperous West and despite the capital moving from Bonn back to Berlin this process is still underway. This was not the only change that Germany would undergo following the upheaval of the Second World War. The Federal Republic of Germany could never have been rebuilt after the war without the help of thousands of Turkish, Moroccan and Tunisian immigrant workers who provided manual labor. Those who remained after the work was done, in particular large numbers of Turkish migrants, have left an indelible mark upon German culture, something which is highlighted by the German's choice of favorite food: the döner kebab, which was invented by a Turkish migrant living in Berlin and has become a national institution.

## Popular traditions and practices

### Weihnachten (viy-nakh-ten)

Weihnachten (Christmas) is a big deal in Germany. Preparations for it begin with the start of advent and most German households count down for the arrival of *das Christkind* (the Christ Child) using a wreath with four candles, an *Adventskrantz,* lighting one candle every Sunday in December leading up to Christmas.

The 6th December is Nikolaustag, a day commemorating Saint Nikolaus. On the evening of the 5th December German children place a boot or show in front of their house door. Overnight the Nikolaus (also called Krampus or Knecht Reprecht) who is similar in appearance to Santa Claus in the USA visits the house and fills the boots with sweets and small presents if the children were well behaved or a bundle of twigs if they were naughty.

During the Christmas period the *Weihnachtsmarkt* (Christmas market) becomes a feature of almost every town and city in German-speaking countries. Craft stalls, entertainment, edible treats and *Glühwein* (literally 'glow-wine') are served. Traditional sweet foods include *Lebkuchen* (Gingerbread), *Stollen* (fruit cake) and *Mazipan*. The most famous of these markets is held in Nürnberg and attracts millions of visitors every year.

Germans traditionally put up their *Weihnachtsbaum* or Christmas tree in the afternoon of the 24th December. On *Heiligabend* (Christmas Eve) a simple meal is served before exchanging gifts, the most popular is potato salad with Frankfurters while other typical meals include fish, duck, fondue or raclette.

**Karneval or Fasching**

Some, but not all, areas of Germany, Austria and Switzerland celebrate *Karneval*, otherwise known as *Fasching*. These festivities occurring before Lent (equivalent to *mardi gras* in other cultures) vary from region to region. Germany's carnival traditions are mostly associated with the Catholic Church and are more prevalent in the country's southern more predominantly Catholic states. Carnival season begins each year on the 11th November at 11:11am and finishes on Ash Wednesday with the main festivities taking place around *Rosenmontag* (Rose Monday). Cologne Carnival is the most famous, although Düsseldorf and Mainz are also centers for celebrations. There are parades in many towns with local authority figures dressed as fools as social convention is turned on its head.

**Ostern**

The Easter Bunny or *Osterhase* is also a tradition in Germany, although in some areas children wait for the *Osterfuchs* or Easter fox instead. Germans love to celebrate the changing of the seasons and often reflect this in the decoration of their homes. Similar to how we decorate a Christmas tree, many German homes decorate the trees and bushes outside their homes with decorated Easter eggs at this time.

**Tanz in den Mai**

In rural areas May Day is celebrated by the lighting of bonfires and the wrapping of a Maibaum or maypole. The old motto *"Tanz in den Mai"* or "Dance into May" has been taken on in modern times and urban areas as a call to celebration and dancing until late in the night before what is a national holiday in Germany.

**Oktoberfest**

When many foreigners think of Germany, it is the typical Oktoberfest scene that they imagine, men and woman in traditional Bavarian dress, drinking beer, singing and swaying along to "oompa band" music. The culture celebrated at Oktoberfest is really more Bavarian than German and this 16 days festival, featuring the largest funfair in the world, is a real celebration of it. Dozens of beer tents are constructed every year on the *Wies'n* or fairground, each serving a different brewery's beer. Most people, including many tourists, wear the traditional *Lederhosen* (leather trousers) for men, while women where traditional Bavarian dress, the *Dirndl*. Things can get a little rowdy and thousands of tourists from all over the world descend on Munich for the festival every year, but if you are in Germany in the autumn then it is an absolute must. Just a word of advice, the *Fest* is not actually in October at all, but in September. The dates were changes many years ago to take advantage of the mild September weather.

**Sylvester**
Almost every country celebrates the New Year, but Germans do it in style. Along with the traditional fireworks and *Sekt* (sparkling wine) at midnight, Germany has some of its very own traditions. Surprising for most English speakers is that nearly all Germans tune in on New Year's Eve to watch the old black and white film *Dinner for One,* about an old woman her butler. Practically unheard of in the UK where it was made it is a cult classic in Germany and no celebration is complete without it!
Another custom is to melt lead over a flame and then look at the shapes the metal makes when it is dropped into a glass of water. The shapes formed are meant to predict your fortune for the year ahead.

Learning German as an English Speaker

As well as sharing similar origins as part of the same family of languages, the English language has also adopted quite a few complete German words. We instantly recognize German foods such as *Bratwurst, Frankfurter, Hamburger, Muesli, Sauerkraut, Strudel* and *Wiener Schnitzel,* as well as the *Lager* or *Schnapps* with which it is washed down.

English-speakers use the word *Rucksack* without even knowing that it is a compound word made up or the words *Ruck-* meaning 'back' and *–sack* meaning 'bag' and we have adapted the verb 'to abseil' from the German verb *sich abseilen*, meaning literally; 'to let oneself down on a rope'.

Some German words have been adopted into English as they brilliantly describe something that we simply have no word for, the words *Doppelgänger, Gemütlichkeit* and *Zeitgeist* are all great examples of these and have made their way into our common vocabulary. As your German vocabulary expands you'll encounter ever more of these.

To Check out the Rest of "*German For Tourists*" Go to Amazon and Look For it Right Now!

## Check Out My Other Books

Are you ready to exceed your limits? Then pick a book from the one below and start learning yet another new language.   I can't imagine anything more fun, fulfilling, and exciting!

If you'd like to see the entire list of language guides (there are a ton more!), go to:

>>http://www.amazon.com/Dagny-Taggart/e/B00K54K6CS/<<

## About the Author

Dagny Taggart is a language enthusiast and polyglot who travels the world, inevitably picking up more and more languages along the way.

Taggart's true passion became learning languages after she realized the incredible connections with people that it fostered. Now she just can't get enough of it. Although it's taken time, she has acquired vast knowledge on the best and fastest ways to learn languages. But the truth is, she is driven simply by her motive to build exceptional links and bonds with others.

She is inspired everyday by the individuals she meets across the globe. For her, there's simply not anything as rewarding as practicing languages with others because she gets to make friends with people from all that come from a variety of cultures. This, in turn, has broadened her mind and thinking more than she would have ever imagined it could.

Of course, as a result of her constant travels, Taggart has become an expert on planning trips and making the most of time spent out of what she calls her "base" town. She jokes that she's practically at the nomad status now, but she's more content to live that way.

She knows how to live on a manageable budget weather she's in Paris or Phnom Penh. She knows how to seek out the adventures and thrills, no doubt, lying in wait at any city she visits. She knows that reflection on each every experience is significant if she wants to grow as a traveler and student of the world's cultures.

Because of this, Taggart chooses to share her understanding of languages and travel so that others, too, can experience the same life-altering benefits she has.

CPSIA information can be obtained at www.ICGtesting.com
Printed in the USA
LVOW09s2309020715

444768LV00022B/717/P